Horace Peters Biddle

American Boyhood

Horace Peters Biddle

American Boyhood

ISBN/EAN: 9783743332119

Manufactured in Europe, USA, Canada, Australia, Japa

Cover: Foto ©ninafisch / pixelio.de

Manufactured and distributed by brebook publishing software (www.brebook.com)

Horace Peters Biddle

American Boyhood

BY

HORACE P. BIDDLE.

"It is opportune to look back upon old times and contemplate our forefathers. Great examples grow thin, and to be fetched from the past world. Simplicity flies away, and iniquity comes at long strides upon us."—SIR THOMAS BROWNE.

PHILADELPHIA:
PUBLISHED FOR THE AUTHOR BY
J. B. LIPPINCOTT & CO.
1876.

Entered, according to Act of Congress, in the year 1875, by

J. B. LIPPINCOTT & CO.,

In the Office of the Librarian of Congress at Washington.

DEDICATION.

TO THE MEMORY
OF THE LATE
THOMAS EWING,
OF OHIO,

WHO WAS A NOBLE SPECIMEN OF AMERICAN BOYHOOD,
AND THE
GREATEST SELF-MADE MAN OF HIS TIME,

THIS POEM IS GRATEFULLY INSCRIBED

BY ONE WHO REVERED THE SAGE AND LOVED THE MAN,

THE AUTHOR.

PREFACE.

The following poem is an attempt to portray American Boyhood, with its surroundings, as it was in the early part of the nineteenth century. It is mainly a picture of country boyhood, because the boyhood of our great cities is more or less exceptional. The muscle, brain, health, and vigor of the nation have been, and must ever be, principally supplied from the great country. Besides, it is the country, and not the city, which forms the character of every free people. It is an effort to represent *National Boyhood*—the boyhood of all sections and of every class—blended into the unity—AMERICAN.

If some of the scenes described appear homely to the present generation, they will be better able to appreciate the advantages they enjoy compared with those possessed by their ancestors, who laid the foundation of their prosperity. But it is difficult, indeed quite impossible, for the present inhabitants, with the privileges they enjoy, to realize the privations endured by the early settlers.

The descriptions in the poem are all taken from real views, and many of them are actual pictures, which, if not sketched soon by some one, must evidently be lost forever.

Incidentally the author sings of our heroes, statesmen, sages, philosophers, poets; of our fathers and mothers,— their trials and struggles, their truth and devotion; of the loves of their sons and daughters,—our brothers and sisters, our friends and neighbors; of freedom and the rights of the human race.

TO THE READER.

These flowers may perish on my tomb,
  And frosts may kill the vine,
Yet they again will spring and bloom
  For other hands to twine;
Or, borne away to other climes,
  They there may live again,
To flourish in far distant times,
  And bear along the strain!

I throw the garland on the stream,
  And trust to other days;
The leaves may die, and yet the theme
  Will bloom in other bays;
But should it wither by the way,
  Or perish on the wave,
Then bring the faded wreath and lay
  It gently on my grave!

CONTENTS.

I.—Proem 15
II.—Home and Parents 18
III.—Childhood and Age 23
IV.—Pioneers and Cabins 30
V.—Homesteads and Social Life 63
VI.—Pursuits and Amusements 76
VII.—Households and Industry 92
VIII.—Schools and Colleges 112
IX.—Churches and Ministers 128
X.—Mills and Distilleries 135
XI.—Artisans and Professions 142
XII.—Prosperity and Hospitality 157
XIII.—Town and Country 172
XIV.—The Continent and its Resources . . . 183
XV.—Reminiscences and Conclusion . . . 194
Notes 205

AMERICAN BOYHOOD.

I.

PROEM.

I.

God! The Eternal, Only One,
   Creator of the All,
Who blessed his work when it was done,
   Gave man this earthly ball;
Creating him in equal right,—
   The world and time his school,—
He gave him knowledge, worth, and might,
   That he the earth might rule!

II.

God rules the universe in love
   To harmonize his plan;
The Lord of all,—below, above,
   Of angel, seraph, man.
He sees alike the sparrow fall
   Or men and angels rise,
And is the Father of us all,
   On earth and in the skies!

III.

So man should rule throughout this world
   In what belongs to man;
Where'er his banner is unfurled
   Unswerving right should reign;

For man is of one brotherhood,
  In body, mind, and soul,—
To do the right, obey the good,
  And love the beautiful!

IV.

America,—the latest found,—
  The last and newest world,
Where Freedom's goddess sits enthroned
  With starry flag unfurled;
And where the laurel strikes its root
  Deep in the native soil,
Untrodden by the tyrant's foot,
  Unrifled by his spoil!

V.

Where Liberty's grand temple stands,
  On mount, in field and wood,
Built high by heroes' daring hands,
  Cemented with their blood,
And consecrated to the race
  With Heaven's approving smile;
No despot's power shall e'er deface
  Or shake the massive pile!

VI.

They boasted not of royal blood,
  These children of the brave,
But claimed the sturdy fatherhood
  That honest parents gave;
And they were not descendants from
  A race whose only worth
Lay with their sires, within the tomb,
  Deep buried in the earth;

VII.

They were the sons of ancestors
    Who filled no coward's place,
But won their liberty in wars
    Waged for the human race;
And, being won, knew how to guard
    It from the tyrant's chain,
And rule without a king or lord,
    By rights which God gave man!

VIII.

God! Man! The grandest thoughts and words
    E'er known to brain or tongue,
Armed with the power of flaming swords
    To smite and conquer wrong,—
To keep us in eternal right,
    And save us from the rod,—
For God needs naught but his own might,
    And man needs naught but God!

II.

HOME AND PARENTS.

IX.

O'er all this earth which God has made,
  No place can be as fair
As where in childhood we have played
  With hearts untouched by care;
On earth hands never built a house,
  Or mansion, castle, dome,
Palace, or throne, as dear to us
  As our own childhood's home!

X.

'Tis where we knew a mother's love,
  Which only once is known,
And where a father toiled and strove
  To shield and guide his son;
Where first the bosom felt its life,—
  So fresh and near its source,
So pure and clear, ere care and strife
  Cast trouble in its course!

XI.

The dear old homestead on the bank,
  The shelter of our birth,—
Though now the weeds grow there so dank,
  The fairest spot on earth;

The roof has crumbled to its fall,
    The mould is on the floor,
The winds are moaning through the wall,
    It is our home no more!

XII.

I tread upon the sunken boards
    And hear no sweet resound;
They shelter now the mouse's hoards,
    And rest upon the ground.
The bats hide in the chimney walls,
    The owls mope on the top,
And, as the evening twilight falls,
    Are ready for the swoop.

XIII.

Another now roams o'er the soil
    Which once our parents trod,
And shares the blessings of their toil
    While they sleep 'neath the sod.
But, ah! it is the human lot,
    As onward roll the years;
Yet still I gaze upon the spot,
    Blinded by filial tears!

XIV.

But still the stream is flowing there,
    The poplar waving high;
The very clouds seem bright and fair:
    They cannot hide the sky;
The birds are singing from the bough
    As in the olden time,
And on the limbs where years ago
    They sang the same sweet chime!

XV.

The leaning maple which we climbed,
    That stood the storm so long,
Where 'neath its branches first we rhymed
    And hid the rustic song,
Bloomed on in broad umbrageous pride,
    And gave us shade at noon,
Till all had gone away or died,
    And that, too, now is gone!

XVI.

No more the stately forests wave,
    The distant hills are bare,
And in the vale there's many a grave;
    Yet men are busy there.
Amidst these scenes we've roamed and played,
    And 'neath their shades have slept;
There first our young hearts loved and prayed,
    And there we laughed and wept!

XVII.

Still stands the house these hands did build
    As young affection's shrine,
Which could not be the home or shield
    Of wife or child of mine;
The scene was changed by the All-Wise
    Who rules us from above,
And builds for us within the skies
    Wiser than human love!

XVIII.

The quiet river still flows on,
    And flowers still bloom and fade,

Leaves spring and wither, then are strown
   Along the vale and glade.
The snows descend and melt away,
   And spring returns again ;
The cloudy and the sunny day
   Still fly o'er hill and plain.

XIX.

The summer, autumn, winter, spring,
   Forever come and go,
And with them take away or bring
   Our happiness and woe.
Around the globe the seasons sweep,
   The night succeeds the day ;
We play and love, we work and weep,
   Then hope, and pass away !

XX.

And in that vale lies buried low
   A household's sacred dust,
Which lived and loved, but rests there now
   In God's eternal trust.
Ah ! who would break the deep repose,—
   So quiet yet so dread,—
Or stir the clods which there inclose
   The ashes of the dead ?

XXI.

How sweet the cherished memories
   Of home and faith and truth,—
The woods and paths, the fields and skies,
   And first fond loves of youth !
How tenderly we felt the ties
   Uniting kindred blood !

Our father then was all that's wise,
  Our mother all that's good!

XXII.

How sweet is hope unto the boy!
  How lithe his active limbs!
How fair the world, how full of joy!
  How blithe life's hill he climbs!
All nature seems to him so bright,—
  The morn that brings the day,
The noon, the evening, and the night,
  The star's undying ray;

XXIII.

The darkness fleeing from the morn,
  The sun's returning blaze,
The flowers that hills and meads adorn,
  The birds upon the sprays;
The harmonies of sight and sound
  On mountain, plain, and sea,
Which, blending with the scenes around,
  Unite the earth and sky.

XXIV.

Ye hills and dales, ye rocks and streams,
  Ye make our bosoms thrill;
And still for thee the tear-drop gleams
  As quivering eyelids fill.
Ye taught us independence, strength,
  And skill in manly strife,
By which to overcome at length
  The dangers of a life!

III.

CHILDHOOD AND AGE.

XXV.

Childhood! in faith so wisely blind,
  To hope and still endure;
Mysterious promise to mankind
  Of God's eternal power;
Having endured, how grand is age,
  In faith so blindly wise,
Looking beyond life's present page,
  Still hoping in the skies!

XXVI.

Rude was the rearing of the boy,
  And sometimes rough the chide;
Yet none the less a mother's joy,
  Nor less the father's pride.
Fed from his mother's own true breast,
  Unspoiled by luxuries,
With well-turned limbs and rounded chest,
  He grew up strong and wise.

XXVII.

His cradle was a wooden trough,
  Rocked by a mother's feet,
And though the couch was hard and rough,
  The sleep was soft and sweet.

The mother with her busy hands
    Would still her labor ply,
And whisper tales of fairy-lands,
    Or sing a lullaby.

XXVIII.

She had no tiny carriage then,
    In those brave hardy times,
To save her little one from pain
    Or spare his tender limbs.
He crept and toddled on right well
    In sunshine or in rain,
And when he hurt himself and fell,
    Got up and tried again.

XXIX.

The springs of health were in his birth,
    His mind had ample page;
They formed the man of truth and worth,
    The hero and the sage.
Through purple veins his generous blood
    Flowed on in ardent tide;
His soul obeyed the true and good,
    To virtuous deeds allied.

XXX.

"The child is father of the *youth*,"
    And so the youth of man;
"Men, children of a larger growth."
    And this completes the span.
Thus would I read the quoted page,
    And so train up the boy;
As was the youth so will be age—
    A country's curse or joy.

XXXI.

A noble boyhood, free and frank,
    A noble manhood makes;
'Tis not the name, nor blood, nor rank,
    That either saves or wrecks.
For all mankind are of one blood,
    Born to a common right;
All have one common Father, God,
    Who rules us in his might!

XXXII.

The older brother's stronger arm
    Aided the younger one,
And kept him safely out of harm
    Until his strength had grown.
And sisters gave their faithful love,
    That nothing could abate,—
A love which angels must approve,—
    Too pure to turn to hate!

XXXIII.

And then our uncles and our aunts,
    And cousins by the score,
Down to the tenth, traced through the haunts
    Of private record lore.
Our grandsires and our great-great-grand,
    The pioneers of fame,
And mothers' mothers through the land,
    Sought out from many a name.

XXXIV.

Grandmothers when they ventured out
    Wore strange, long-fingered gloves,

Grandfathers donned their well-saved coat,
  All wrinkled into grooves.
The aged folk drew round the hearth,
  Old ladies sat and knit;
Old gentlemen talked of their birth,
  And aired their ancient wit.

XXXV.

The time-stained sampler, still preserved,
  Which our grandmothers worked
With strange devices, crossed and curved,
  Wherein sweet thoughts still lurked;
Where sentiments could still be read
  Of hearts that loved in youth,
And early stories of the dead,
  Whose souls had found the truth!

XXXVI.

Old-fashioned mothers of the day,
  Whose hands, though hard with toil,
Soft as the touch of angels lay
  Upon the brow, whose smile
Could make us happy in our tears,
  Whose words could reconcile
Us to our pain, banish our fears,
  And all our woes beguile!

XXXVII.

The mothers of America,—
  Of soldier and of sage,
Who bore our flag to victory,
  And quelled the lightning's rage;
Of heroes to defend the soil,—
  A firm, united band;

And hardy sons of honest toil,
    Whose labors blessed the land.

XXXVIII.

The mother of our Washington,
    Mary! Oh, sacred name!
Abiah bore our wisest son,
    Who won from heaven his fame.
And humbler mothers bore brave sons,
    And daughters pure and fair,—
Worthy as those who reign on thrones
    Or crowns of jewels wear.

XXXIX.

Our plain, old-fashioned fathers were
    Upright and honest men;
To keep them in their dealings fair
    They needed not the pen.
Their simple word was note or bond,
    And stronger than the law,
Or all that judges can expound
    To hold the world in awe!

XL.

True honesty their bosoms warmed,
    And Justice they adored,
Their obligations were performed
    Without her scales or sword.
Gentle, although their garbs were rude,
    Tried friends in woe or weal;
Tender, affectionate, and good,
    They felt all hearts can feel!

XLI.

How strong and wise their native minds!
  How true and warm their hearts!
Their conduct needed not the blinds
  Of petty hidden arts.
They openly expressed their thoughts,
  As candid as in youth;
They knew no schemes, and had no plots,
  But trusted all to truth!

XLII.

Yet still remained a very few
  Brave, grand, old gentlemen,
Who wore knee-buckles and a queue,
  And loved King George's reign;
And here and there a proud patroon
  Who bore the people hate,
Believing more in sceptered crown
  Than in the equal state.

XLIII.

Our fathers ruled, their sons obeyed,
  With all their manly powers,
And daughters made their mothers glad,—
  As beautiful as flowers.
And friend to friend was firm as steel,
  Lovers were true and fond;
Heart beat to heart, and each could feel
  A faithful heart respond!

XLIV.

Perchance along the shores of time
  There linger yet a few

Who lived in days of deeds sublime,
    When our broad land was new,
To tell us o'er the tales of youth,
    Forgetting they are old,—
The tales of courage, love, and truth,
    Which years ago were told!

IV.

PIONEERS AND CABINS.

XLV.

The wigwam stood through ages past
    Amidst the forest scene,
Or near the lakes and prairies vast,
    With broad and sunny sheen.
The missionary came and shared
    The shelter of the wild,
And fared as his red brother fared,—
    The forest's native child.

XLVI.

Next came the tent—like snowy swan,
    Pitched for a single night—
Of bold explorer, who at dawn
    Again took up his flight.
And then the hunter built his camp
    Near valley, stream, or bay;
At night the wood-fire was his lamp,
    The sun his guide by day.

XLVII.

Ere long the treaty-making power
    And chieftains had "a talk";
Soon after, the surveyor's corps
    Trailed on their weary walk.

And when the Indians had grown tame
  The "squatter" claimed his home;
At length the thrifty settler came
  To build a prouder dome.

XLVIII.

On the broad prairie's treeless space
  They sometimes dug a cave,
And built a mound that marked the place
  High o'er the gopher's grave;
But soon the shanty's single room
  Displayed its lowly roof,
And there ere long the locust's bloom
  Waved in the breeze aloof.

XLIX.

The Indian trail wound through the woods,
  O'er prairie, hill, and vale,
Below the mount, above the floods,
  Around the gulch and dale,
Along the high dividing ridge
  Where gurgling streams arose,
By shallow ford or rocky bridge,
  To watch their wily foes.

L.

By hill and stream the white man's trace
  Was blazed from tree to tree,
Marked by high points from place to place,
  That weary eyes might see
The towering peak, far on the way,
  And high above the woods,
Lighted by morn and evening ray,
  Parting the gilded clouds!

LI.

Tree after tree, mile after mile,
    O'er towering shrubs and flowers,
Stretching afar o'er plain and hill,
    Through thickets, grubs, and bowers;
Home of the weird and wonderful,
    Of serpent, beast, and bird,
O'erawing man's immortal soul
    With God's unwritten word.

LII.

Amidst the dark, deep, solemn woods,
    Shutting away the sky,—
Fit temple for the ancient gods,
    Ere man had looked on high,—
Was often heard the panther's yell,
    Or eagle's piercing scream,
That echoed from the rock and dell,
    Breaking the sombre dream.

LIII.

Yet oft the wilds in milder moods
    By gentler tones were stirred,
While tinkling rills and murmuring floods
    Rung out their rich accord;
And Zephyr sent the wooing breeze
    To greet the fragrant flowers,
And whisper to the bending trees
    Of summer's genial showers.

LIV.

The dove's sweet coo at morn was heard,
    At eve the whip-poor-will,

And chirping songs from many a bird
    O'er flowery dale and hill.
Gay butterflies—sweet wingéd flowers—
    And evening's flying stars
Sported away their summer hours,
    Lighting the wild parterres!

LV.

All nations came. Their strongest men
    Fled far from tyranny—
Gaul, Saxon, Celt, Swede, German, Dane—
    To join our liberty.
True men of courage, nerve, and bone
    Sought out the forest land;
The races mingling into one,—
    A brave, heroic band.

LVI.

The pioneer pushed on his way
    Deep in the forest's shade.
And after many a weary day
    The firm foundations laid
Of home and independence, worth,
    Security and rest,
And lived to send descendants forth,
    Fulfilling God's behest.

LVII.

How many weary "flittings" came
    From North, and South, and East,
With creaking wheels and worn-out team,
    Seeking the great Northwest.
Their single-trees were lashed with withes
    To keep them in their place,

And oft odd hooks found at the smith's
Eked out a hempen trace.

LVIII.

Sometimes loose collars made of straw,
　　And hames of cracked sticks,
With barken bands and straps to draw,
　　Made up the *shackly* fix.
They cut their way and struggled on
　　Without a trace or road,
And bore their "plunder" up and down,
　　Each one his weary load.

LIX.

The father marched with axe and gun,
　　The mother with the babe,
The team was managed by the son;
　　The oldest daughter, Mabe,
With little sister on her hip,
　　Across the sloughy mud,
As agile as a doe, would skip,
　　Or wade the wider flood.

LX.

Perchance the little babe grew ill,
　　And sickened by the way;
They prayed to God's most holy will
　　To keep it from the clay.
Another day perchance it died;
　　Then, near the forest road,
By rock, or stream, 'twas lowly laid
　　And left alone with God!

LXI.

Some born, perchance, upon the way,
    Beneath the spreading tree,
Where first they saw the light of day
    Reflected from the sky;
For God was there to bless the birth
    And soothe a mother's care,
To give another soul to earth
    And dry the infant's tear!

LXII.

The children strong enough to walk
    Were not allowed to ride:
They trudged along, full of their talk,
    And followed well their guide;
But when they forded pond or stream
    They climbed the horses' backs;
The helpless ones—hauled by the team—
    Were snuggled in like packs.

LXIII.

The patient cow supplied their milk,
    And helped to bear the load;
With soft mild eye, and lash like silk,—
    Too gentle for the goad.
The timid ewes, and lazy hog,
    And noisy calves that lowed,
Were guarded by the faithful dog,
    And guided on their road.

LXIV.

On horseback oft they swam the streams,
    Daring the swelling tide,

And, ox or horse, they crossed their teams
    By swimming side by side;
Then, piece by piece, they bore their goods,
    And wagon, wheel by wheel,
Upon a raft high o'er the floods,
    With bold, untiring zeal.

LXV.

Sometimes one horse was all they had,
    Then they would "ride and tie,"
And weary legs would leap right glad
    To see the horse hard by.
Perchance by turns they walked and rode,
    Yet traveled side by side;
Fast friends they were, through wood or flood,
    Whatever ill betide.

LXVI.

The girls and boys, the lambs and ewes,
    The mother and the child,—
All huddled in the narrow close
    Wherein the goods were piled,—
Were placed upon the venturous bark,—
    With guns and axes stowed,—
And, like the chosen of the ark,
    Across the waters rode.

LXVII.

They oft slept shelterless at night
    Beneath God's canopy;
What though the moon withheld her light?
    The stars were bright on high.

Perchance the night portended storms,—
    The wagon formed a tent,
Which to their weary, shiv'ring forms
    Its scanty covering lent.

LXVIII.

What though the house of logs was built,
    And yet was but a pen?
It was no dome concealing guilt,
    But home that sheltered men.
What though it had no roof nor floor,
    Save 'twas the bison's skin?
With blanket for the pane and door?
    It let the wanderer in.

LXIX.

How glad to reach a camp or shed,
    Or friendly cabin door,
Where, if they could not have a bed,
    They bundled on the floor!
Fair girls invited 'neath the quilt
    Did modestly accept,
And, free from danger as from guilt,
    There innocently slept!

LXX.

The forest cabins of the land
    Were low and humble-roofed,
The staircase was a ladder, and
    The chamber was a loft;
And built from sleeper to the peak
    Without a screw or nail;

There was no iron—bolt nor spike—
  From ridgepole to the sill.

LXXI.

At first they firm foundation laid
  With four great heavy logs,
Of white-oak, if it could be had,
  Or cypress from the bogs.
The handspike rolled them to the place,—
  Of beech or dogwood cut,—
And thus they formed a lasting base
  Upon the chosen spot.

LXXII.

The best and straightest trees were cut,
  For lastingness and strength,—
The logs all peeled, squared at the butt
  Exactly of a length;
Thus, notched and saddled to a scribe,
  And every corner plumbed,
They built the cabin, barn, and crib,
  Where long the wilds had bloomed.

LXXIII.

Whene'er the walls were up so high
  They could not reach the top,
They put up poles, peeled, smooth, and dry,
  To form a gentle slope;
Then laid the logs on longer skids,
  And pushed them up with forks;
And many were the dangerous slides,
  The slips, and sudden jerks.

LXXIV.

Eave-bearers, butting-poles, and knees,
    With weight-poles, held the roof;
The heavy floor, split out of trees,
    Itself was weight enough.
A cave was dug hard by the hearth
    To keep the winter sauce;
The puncheons that concealed the earth
    Rested on sticks across.

LXXV.

They hewed the cabins down inside—
    Unlike the hasty booth—
The rough, uneven knots to hide,
    And make the walls more smooth.
The upper joists were merely poles,
    The walls were chinked and daubed;
Sometimes the windows were but holes,
    Yet they were seldom robbed.

LXXVI.

The door on wooden hinges hung,
    Which formed the battens, too,
And they on wooden brackets swung;
    Outside it had a bow,
Thumb-piece, or string, to lift the latch
    Which always let us in;
To hold it firmly in the catch
    'Twas fastened by a pin.

LXXVII.

Two round, straight sticks, with two ends crossed,
    And two fast in the wall,

A bedstead made—a fork the post—
  That would not move nor fall.
The boys slept just beneath the roof,
  The girls in trundle-bed,
The little baby in its trough,
  Close by its mother's head.

LXXVIII.

The good old-fashioned chimney-place
  Took up almost one side;
A score could stand within the space,
  It was so high and wide.
They rolled the heavy back-log in,
  And laid the forestick down,
Then dropped the kindlings in between,
  And threw the top-log on;

LXXIX.

Next laid the billets on criss-cross,—
  A half a wagon-load,—
Then soon the curling smoke arose
  And sent its clouds abroad.
Ere long burst forth the cheerful flames,
  While coals fell down below,
And heated back-wall, hearth, and jambs,
  Which long retained their glow.

LXXX.

The back-log lay hard by the door,
  All ready to put on;
They rolled it in across the floor,
  And o'er the resting-stone.

They brought the kindling in at night,
   And laid it by the jamb,
At morn the buried brand so bright
   Soon lighted up the flame.

LXXXI.

Sometimes they had cast-iron dogs
   To lay the forestick on,
But branches smaller than the logs,
   In front, lay on the stone.
Once when a boy—and such a sight
   I never shall forget—
I saw brass dogs, and, oh! so bright,
   Upon a hearth-stone set!

LXXXII.

Some neither tongs nor shovel had,—
   They used a poking-stick,
And board shaped like a shovel-blade,
   With handle long and thick.
The iron shovel and the tongs,
   Which mate so socially,
But seldom joined their clink with songs,
   Or rattled in the glee.

LXXXIII.

On high they placed a chimney-pole,
   On which the trammel hung,
With hook and slide and many a hole
   To gauge the height it swung.
They sometimes used a wooden crane
   Made of a sapling's crotch,

To which they hung a piece of chain,
    Or wooden hook with notch.

LXXXIV.

And when the orchard bore its fruit
    There strings of apples hung,
Out of the way of smoke and soot,
    And kettle as it swung.
We dried our peaches on a kiln,
    Or round the fire on boards,
Or sometimes took them to the still
    And made a drink for lords.

LXXXV.

If overnight they lost their fire,
    They struck the steel and flint,
And, like the one who roused Jove's ire,
    Soon stole the hasty glint;
Or to the nearest neighbor ran
    The glowing coal to fetch,
Or with the gunlock flashed the pan
    Until the tow would catch.

LXXXVI.

With tinder-box to light the pipe,
    Or knife and flint, with punk,
The blazing sparks would flash and skip,
    And kindle leaf and chunk.
When first the friction-match was made
    They thought it very well,
But still the old man shook his head
    And used his flint and steel.

LXXXVII.

They piled the winter wood-pile high,
    Like log-heaps on the field,
With maul and wedge and axe hard by
    To make the crotches yield.
From field and clearing wood was "snaked,"
    And split to smallest size,
To heat the oven when they baked
    The wheaten loaf and pies.

LXXXVIII.

The oven with its roof so high,
    To keep it out of reach
Of heat and flame, was built hard by
    The ash-heap and the leach.
The work-bench and the shaving-horse
    Sometimes stood 'neath a shed,
But oftener in the great out-doors,
    Beneath the overhead.

LXXXIX.

There were a few cast-iron stoves,—
    They came in separate plates,
All made to fit like tongues and grooves,
    With doors that swung like gates.
They did not show the dancing rays,
    But stood in sombre gloom;
They warmed us, but we missed the blaze
    That made a cheerful room.

XC.

Ah! many a cabin in its day,
    Built roughly in the woods,

With chimney walls of cat-and-clay,
    Withstood the storms and floods;
And from its hearth of native ground,
    And floor so thick and stout,
Sent forth its blessing far around,
    With latch-string always out.

XCI.

Its cheering light shone on the oak
    As night crept o'er the hill,
High rose the fitful sparks and smoke
    While all the world was still.
Beneath the spangled canopy
    It stood in sweet repose,
And soon as morning kissed the sky
    With strength renewed we rose.

XCII.

We watched the order in the sky,
    Guiding the stars so true,
And heard a soft, sweet harmony
    Trembling along the blue.
We knew not how the orbs were rolled,
    Nor why the sky was fair,
But the eternal Spirit told
    Us God was reigning there!

XCIII.

We gazed upon the sky and felt
    A deep religious awe;
There goodness, truth, and beauty dwelt
    In harmony and law.

United there for aye they reign,
  Shining from star to star,
To light and guide the souls of men
  That live forever there!

XCIV.

The bird's first chirp, or cock's shrill horn,
  So sweet, so loud and clear,
Awoke us with the coming morn
  To meet the bracing air.
The hen and chicks that feared the hawk
  Came out at peep of day;
Then, too, we heard the duck's hoarse squawk,
  And gander's roundelay.

XCV.

The snowy lambs, as fleet as fawns,
  Strayed from their mother's side,
To skip along the grassy lawns
  At morn and eventide.
When missed, the ewe's uneasy bleat
  Soon called them from their play,
And then, alarmed, they came as fleet
  As they had fled away.

XCVI.

And when the spring was well assured,
  The noisy frog's clear peep,
Or owl's wild hoot at twilight heard,
  Oft chased away our sleep.
In summer-time, along the shore
  Of larger ponds and streams,

The bull-frog's *chug*, or bellowing roar,
    At night disturbed our dreams.

XCVII.

The compass steered the venturous prow
    And marked the forest trace ;
The axe, the mattock, and the plow
    Subdued the wilderness.
The frontier settler broke the field
    And tilled the virgin soil,
So ready in its wealth to yield
    The rich reward of toil.

XCVIII.

He planted corn among the logs,
    And hoed it as they lay,
And gathered grass along the bogs
    To make his winter hay.
In summer-time wide was the range
    Where cattle went and came,
The farm was nature's mighty grange,
    Stretching o'er dale and stream.

XCIX.

The straggling fence ran o'er the ridge
    Round many a tree and root,
While fallen timber formed a bridge
    To cross the streams on foot.
The zigzag pannels round the field
    Preserved the growing corn,
Eked out by tree-tops as a shield
    'Gainst cunning hoof and horn.

C.

The bar-share-plow first broke the ground,
    And, if the soil was clay,
It took ten rods to turn it round,
    And almost half the day.
But soon the "bull-plow" took its place,
    Made from an iron mould,
Which, packed afar by "Zane's Trace,"
    Was first at Pittsburg rolled.

CI.

They plowed the corn with shovel-plow,
    And, if 'twas rooty ground,
It cost the plowman many a vow,
    It jerked him so around.
With these and wooden harrow-teeth
    Stuck in a wooden fork,
Eke hempen rope and hickory withe,
    The farmer plied his work.

CII.

And in the fall the friendly mast,
    That fell from laden bough,
Through half the winter months would last,
    Retrieved from 'neath the snow.
As nature fed the wandering beast
    O'er mountain, vale, and plain,
Domestic animals could feast,
    And then return to man.

CIII.

The men took rifles to the field,
    Shot-pouch and powder-horn,

To have them ready as a shield
    While they were hoeing corn;
Perchance to kill a wandering buck,
    A panther, or a bear,
Or pick a turkey from the flock,
    Should either come too near.

CIV.

At home the rifle hung on hooks
    Above the mantel-piece;
'Twas always charged for game outlooks
    And ready for the chase.
The shot-pouch, made of panther's pelt,
    And horn, hung at its breech;
The tomahawk, with knife and belt,
    Was handy to the reach.

CV.

The rifle, tomahawk, and knife
    Conquered the prowling beast,
From savages protected life,
    And won the means to feast.
The froe, the auger, and the saw
    Completed roof and door;
The ballot-box and common law
    Held all their rights secure.

CVI.

They all turned out to work the road,—
    Man, horse, boy, colt, and team,—
To plow the earth, and haul the load,
    And bridge the slough and stream.
The hill and quagmire to avoid
    They dug, and ditched, and drained;

They graveled and they *corduroyed*,
    And felled the trees that leaned.

CVII.

Sewers were made of hollow logs,
    And laid beneath the roads
To lead the water from the bogs;
    O'er which the heaviest loads
On wheels and sleds were safely hauled
    Where once strong horses stuck,
And e'en with empty wagons stalled
    Amidst quicksand and muck.

CVIII.

They built their bridges over streams
    On cribs or wooden pens,
Filled full of stones, with long oak beams
    That rested at their ends.
The middle stretch was swung on hooks
    Of wood from plates high o'er
The swollen waves, and hung in yokes
    To hold the puncheon floor.

CIX.

Across the runs and narrow rills,
    And gullies, drains, and holes,
From bank to bank they laid their sills
    And made a floor of poles.
They had no derricks, hoisting-cranes,
    Snatch-blocks, nor tackles then;
The work was done without machines,
    By strength of mighty men.

CX.

They gave the boy the poorest tool
    That was amongst the band,
Then bade him dig or chop and roll,
    And make a full work-hand.
With what a high, ambitious pride
    He felt himself a man!
How pleased he was the ox to guide,
    Or drive the fiery span!

CXI.

For many years there were no roads
    In all the country round,
Save those they made of earth and sods,
    Where broad, rich lands abound.
Once in the road, the story ran,
    (I vouch not for its source,)
They found a hat,—'twas on a man,—
    And 'neath the man, a horse!

CXII.

We heard of stone-pikes far away,
    Scaled in the rocky peaks,
Winding around the mountains gray,
    Where rosy morning breaks;
But made our own of mud and clay,
    Our *corduroy* of wood,
And caved the sloping hill away
    To shun the swamp and flood.

CXIII.

And oft we traveled without roads
    By section, township, range,

Afar away through thickest woods,
   So dreary, wild, and strange,
And never missed the mount or stream,—
   Encamping for the night,
And dreaming many a pleasing dream
   Ere morn returned the light.

CXIV.

They dug into the ancient mounds
   Which time could not efface,
Supposed to be the burying-grounds
   Of some forgotten race;
And there they found—strange sight to see—
   Rude implements, big bones,
Charcoal, and bits of pottery,
   And human skeletons;

CXV.

And o'er the lower plains and fields
   They found flint arrow-heads,
With smooth, broad stones, like warriors' shields,
   And pebbles bored like beads,
And shells, as well as flints and stones,
   For ornament or use;
Some found alone, some with the bones
   Of mastodon or moose.

CXVI.

And some rude specimens of arts
   Were found in bog and mire.
They made their gun-flints of the darts
   To strike the rifle's fire;
The clumsy pan, with powder primed,
   From *frizzen* caught the spark,

And hanging fire, unless well timed,
    They missed the game or mark.

CXVII.

They also found the tomahawk
    And Indian scalping-knife,
Abandoned in the battle's shock
    Or lost amidst the strife;
And oft plowed up old rusted guns,
    And swords, of English make,
On battle-fields, or with the bones
    Where stood the fatal stake.

CXVIII.

The red man lingered near the lands
    That held his fathers' bones,
On hills, in swamps, on plains, in sands,
    Unmarked by graves or stones;
His name still known by stream or place
    Near which he was entombed;
But, ah! no care can save his race:
    In spite of man 'tis doomed!

CXIX.

His dusky daughters and his sons
    Were driven west,—still west,—
Afar away from homes and thrones,
    On plain and mountain-crest;
His heart was buried in the graves
    That made their common tomb;
The chieftain could not rouse his braves,
    For fate had sealed their doom.

CXX.

The music of the woodman's blow,
　　Resounding through the vale,
High o'er the murmuring streamlet's flow,
　　Began another tale.
The bear, the wolf, and panther fled,
　　In distant wilds to roam;
The deer, of man much less afraid,
　　Soon gathered round his home.

CXXI.

The eagle, screaming, left the wood,
　　And proudly soared away;
It was no more a place of blood,
　　Nor quarry for his prey.
The dove, the robin, and the quail,
　　Hard by man's dwelling-place,
Cooed, sang, and whistled in the vale,
　　And built their nests in peace.

CXXII.

The woodman smote the lofty tree,
　　And bid the monarch fall—
The stoutest knight of chivalry
　　Could not wield axe or maul.
Around him soon he prostrate laid
　　The mighty of the woods;
No braver hero with his blade
　　E'er dared the fields and floods.

CXXIII.

Gems never shone with nobler glow
　　On diadem or crown,

Than drops of sweat upon his brow,
    So manly, broad, and brown.
No head e'er held a sounder brain,
    Nor breast a truer heart;
No firmer limbs e'er bore the strain
    Of honest labor's part.

CXXIV.

What though no learning filled his head?
    'Twas full of strong clear sense;
What though no court his manners bred?
    He was a native prince.
Simple in conduct and in deed,
    And gentle in his words,
The *man* in all he did and said
    Made him the peer of lords!

CXXV.

For him no garden yet had smiled
    With fruitful plant or rose,
Nor mansion yet its walls had piled,
    Inviting to repose;
But there was beauty in the wilds,
    And shelter in the bower,
And riven oak a fragrance yields
    As sweet as fruit or flower.

CXXVI.

The primal duty he obeyed,
    To dress and till the land,
And by his labor earned his bread,
    Fulfilling God's command.
At morn he took the frugal meal,
    Prepared with loving care;

At noontide in the shady dell
   He shared the wholesome fare.

CXXVII.

With hollowed hand to form a cup,
   Or leaf of sycamore,
He drew the crystal waters up
   From nature's endless store;
Or prostrate on the pebbly brink,
   As on the wavelet laughed,
He bowed with thirsty lips to drink
   The cool, refreshing draught.

CXXVIII.

The forests fell beneath their stroke,
   The rocks were shaped to use,
The well-matched steers bowed to their yoke,
   The horse obeyed the noose;
The logs and chunks and brush were piled
   Upon the new-made field,
The "truck-patch" and the garden smiled
   As lands were brought to yield.

CXXIX.

Ah! many a noble timber-tree
   Was deadened as it stood:
The only way the land to free
   From overgrowth of wood;
And when they fell, the trunk or top
   Oft broke the fence in gaps;
We "niggered" those too large to chop,
   Then rolled and "snaked" the heaps.

CXXX.

The clearing soon was green with corn
  Amidst the girdled trees;
We worked it in the dewy morn
  And in the evening breeze.
The bloomy lint we used to pull,
  And thrash the seedy bolls;
We washed the fleece and sheared the wool
  That made the snowy rolls.

CXXXI.

The wool was carded by machine,
  The drum and band its rig,
With upright shaft, so long and thin,
  And wheel like whirligig.
The bank o'ertopped the sharp mill-roof
  Which seemed to touch its side;
We sent the bundles from aloof,
  Slipping them down the guide.

CXXXII.

We broke and scutched the fibrous flax
  With many a sturdy blow,
And made it ready for the racks
  By hackling out the tow.
The daughters picked the cotton-wool
  Until no seed remained,
And then to make the bat and roll
  They carded it by hand.

CXXXIII.

We also raised and broke our hemp
  For halter, trace, and rope,

To hamper beasts hard by the camp,
   And keep them in their scope.
The rope-walk ran beneath the trees :
   Three wooden spindles turned
To spin and twist the strands in threes,—
   An art that many learned.

CXXXIV.

Then came the noisy spinning-wheel
   Which took up so much room ;
The whirling swifts, the snapping reel,
   The warping bars and loom.
The little wheel to spin the flax
   To seven hundred fine,
And tow, much coarser, for the sacks,
   Or twist it into twine.

CXXXV.

Ah ! many a time I tied their bands,
   The spinners to annoy ;
The fair ones then would seize my hands
   And rap them with the " boy ";
And oft I tangled up their yarn
   Like fairy, elf, or witch,
Then fled to garret or to barn
   To 'scape the tingling switch.

CXXXVI.

They bleached the linen o'er the lawn,
   As smoothly spread it lay,
By sprinkling it at early dawn,
   And through the sunny day.
And 'twas a lovely sight to see
   The maidens' rosy feet—

And ankles—in their liberty,
  Flashing amidst the heat.

CXXXVII.

They colored drab with white-ash bark,
  And brown with butternut,
With oak a tint more rich and dark,
  And black with walnut-root;
With home-grown madder colored red,
  Then mixed the black and white,
Or red and blue; and, thread for thread,
  Our socks and mittens knit;

CXXXVIII.

Or sheared the black sheep of the flock,
  And mixed with white his fleece,
To knit the mitten and the sock,
  Or weave the mottled piece.
We sometimes sheared the early lambs,
  And sold the wool for hats;
Or, with the clippings from their dams,
  Carded it into bats.

CXXXIX.

Fair women then picked, carded, spun,
  And wove the cotton-wool;
And when their honest work was done
  They thought it beautiful.
At length ingenious cotton-gins
  Suggested other hints,
Until a thousand quick machines
  Made dimities and prints.

CXL.

No silk nor satin spun by worms,
    Nor cambric,—white as snow,—
Nor royal purple, clothed their forms;
    Their best was calico,
Or gingham for a Sunday dress,
    And modesty their charm,
While flannel from the home-made piece
    In winter kept them warm.

CXLI.

The men all joined as if but one
    To help a neighbor through
With what he could not do alone,
    Yet what they all could do;
And all together neighbored round:
    No one received a slight;
Howe'er they differed, all felt bound
    To stand by common right.

CXLII.

And the new-comer found a home
    Where'er a cabin stood,
Till he could build his own rude dome
    Still deeper in the wood.
He chopped his logs and cleared his ground,
    Which gave his cattle browse,
Then neighbors came from miles around
    To help him raise his house.

CXLIII.

The weary traveler put up
    At cabin, camp, or shed,

Where'er he found a household group,
    As on his pathway led ;
He shared their shelter and their bread,
    In friendship's truest guise,
Nor asked permission, for he read
    His welcome in their eyes.

CXLIV.

Their friendship, favor, love, and truth
    Followed not fame nor wealth ;
In age, through manhood, from their youth,
    Too strong and brave for stealth.
Unfed, unclothed, none left their door
    For want of scrip or pelf;
While with them ever were the poor,
    They never thought of self.

CXLV.

And if a neighbor's house was burned,
    The news flew far and wide ;
He with his nearest friend sojourned
    Until he was supplied.
They brought him food, and clothes, and pelf,—
    Whate'er they had in store ;
And oftentimes he found himself
    Far richer than before.

CXLVI.

Whate'er misfortune fell upon
    Their friends or neighborhood,
They all would do what could be done
    To save from fire and flood.
In sickness they provided needs
    To cure and cheer the weak ;

Their sympathy expressed in deeds
  What words can never speak—

CXLVII.

The sympathy of nature's touch,
  That wakes the heart's best chords,
Which promised naught yet did so much,—
  Too deep and full for words.
The logic of the polished Greek,
  The wisdom of the seer,
And all that eloquence can speak,
  Must yield to nature's tear.

CXLVIII.

When death struck down strong men or babes
  And set the spirit free,
They made their coffins of the slabs
  Split from the forest-tree;
With withes and saplings made a bier,
  And bore them to the grave;
Rude was the scene, yet God was there
  The deathless soul to save.

CXLIX.

Brave men! They met what fortune gave,
  And used at their command
What means they had, to conquer, save,
  And beautify the land.
And when at last their strength succumbed,
  They died as heroes die,
And 'midst the rocks and wilds entombed,
  Slept sweetly 'neath the sky.

CL.

And round the scenes where loved ones lay—
    While eyes were wet and dim—
They set the poplar's budding spray,
    That grew so tall and slim;
The willow also there did wave,
    Drooping so tenderly;
The one seemed pointing to the grave,
    The other to the sky!

V.

HOMESTEADS AND SOCIAL LIFE.

CLI.

After the round-log cabin rose
   With clapboard roof and shed,
They raised the larger hewed-log house
   With shingle roof instead.
And then framed houses soon appeared,
   With lath-and-plaster walls;
Their gaudy parapets were reared
   High o'er their spacious halls.

CLII.

Yet still the cabin stood hard by,
   Sometimes as kitchen used,
Or place to keep the kindlings dry,
   Or where the tools were housed;
Perchance the shelter for a crop
   Of pumpkins, flax, or peas,
Or turned into a shed or shop
   For work on rainy days.

CLIII.

Stone houses, too, with rubble walls,
   Might here and there be seen,
With name and date scratched on in scrawls,
   And on the top a vane;

Brick mansions now and then were built
   In some rich neighborhood,
All pedigreed in letters gilt,
   To show how long they'd stood.

CLIV.

Huge barns were set in sloping banks,
   And on rough, solid walls,
With cattle-sheds along their flanks,
   And stables, bins, and stalls.
They held the wheat and oats in sheaves,
   Also the hay and straw,
And saved the fodder—stalks and leaves—
   To fill the bovine maw.

CLV.

A covered way and double door,
   That opened high and wide,
Led up into the thrashing-floor,
   With mows on either side.
The teams went in with loads of grain,
   Or jags of new-mown hay,
All sheltered from the fitful rain
   That cooled the summer day.

CLVI.

The barns' red sides, kissed by the sun,
   Gave back the glancing ray,
And o'er the hills and valleys shone
   For miles and miles away.
High o'er their peaks the weather-cocks
   Displayed their painted crests,
And 'neath their eaves the pigeon-box
   Hung near the swallows' nests.

CLVII.

And oft the barn was built before
  The mansion was put up,
That they might sell the garnered store
  And clear a larger scope;
For frugal farmers would reside
  In their old cabin homes
Until the fertile fields were wide,
  Then build their prouder domes.

CLVIII.

Then came our parties, cordial, free
  From all suspicious watch;
They told our fortunes by the tea,
  And "guessed" at many a match.
The future they could read full well
  By grounds within the cup,
Yet more by blushes they could tell
  Which ones were "sitting up."

CLIX.

And rural plays of various kinds,—
  The apple-cuttings, where,
By snapping seeds and throwing rinds,
  We teased the blushing fair.
And by the gown on Sunday eve,
  Or coat worn by the beau,
We knew who would not take their leave
  Till morning stars would glow.

CLX.

We watched the seasons come and go,
  And counted every day,

And wondered why they came so slow
   And flew so quick away.
But, as the sun that lights the dome
   Must soon sink down in night,
Our pleasures ever slowly come,
   And quickly take their flight.

CLXI.

The wooden clock without a case,
   Screwed fast against the wall,
Recorded time's unending pace,
   Unheeding great and small.
We watched the swinging pendulum,
   And wondered at the bell,
And how the moon could go and come,
   All keeping time so well.

CLXII.

A noon-mark often set the time
   With sunlight from the sky,
To regulate the mid-day chime
   With moon and stars on high.
Some had a silver watch and chain,
   But these were very rare;
Gold watches were so seldom seen
   They made the rustics stare.

CLXIII.

Their furniture they thought was good,—
   A box, a trunk, or chest;
The cupboard in the corner stood,
   A bureau was their best.
A fall-leaf table, moved by hand,
   Or round one, set aside;

A rocking-chair and sewing-stand
   Attained their highest pride.

CLXIV.

The bedstead had its huge, tall post,
   So high that to get on
You had to climb, then you were lost
   Amidst the feathery down.
They made the stool, split-bottom chair,
   And bench to sit upon ;
The windsor-seat was very rare,
   Upholstery quite unknown.

CLXV.

The dresser had its spoons notched in
   The front edge of the shelves,
The cups and saucers and the tin
   Seemed piled as if by elves;
They were so mixed and cobbled up
   'Twas difficult to tell
Which was the saucer, bowl, or cup,—
   And yet arranged so well.

CLXVI.

Few were the carpets on their floors,
   The boards were scrubbed with sand ;
No paint was on the sills or doors,
   They rubbed them clean by hand.
Sometimes within their best spare rooms
   Rag carpets might be seen,—
A trouble to the hickory brooms
   To keep them neat and clean.

CLXVII.

In winter evenings round the fire,
  During the storm and cold,
We piled the blazing fuel higher,
  And many a story told;
With kisses, jokes, and nuts to crack,
  And apples, cider, flip,
We feasted with a hearty smack
  That tingled tongue and lip.

CLXVIII.

The glowing wood-fire on the hearth,
  The tumbling brand and sparks,
The flashing light and genial mirth,
  Invited sly remarks;
While fitful shadows on the walls—
  Distorting face and form,
Like Hadean shades dressed in their palls—
  Threw round a wild, weird charm.

CLXIX.

The bright, warm flames, their whispering tones,
  The thoughts of dangers past,
The safety of our cherished ones,
  The shelter from the blast,
While storms were raging in the sky,
  Awoke within the breast
A sense of sweet security,
  That calmed and soothed our rest.

CLXX.

Besides the light from beechen chip
  Or hickory bark, we had

A turnip lamp and " slut" or dip
    To make the evening glad.
We made our lamp-wick of a rag,
    A twisted husk, or string,
Then hung the light on nail or peg,
    And let it shine and swing.

CLXXI.

How very bashful we were then!
    How very awkward, too!
We felt ourselves as brave as men,
    And yet afraid to woo.
The virtues of the sterner sex
    Were such as most endure,
The beauty that did so perplex
    Was womanly and pure.

CLXXII.

And with our sleighs in winter-time,
    The jumper and the sled,
And cow-bells with their noisy chime,
    How merrily we sped!
The horses, restive 'neath the chafe,
    Were smoking with their heat;
The girlish scream, and ringing laugh,
    Proclaimed the overset.

CLXXIII.

The rustic ball, a " frolic" called,
    The dance on puncheon floor,
The music on a bench installed,—
    One fiddle, and no more.
They danced till coming day would peep
    In giddy run and whirl;

All artless was the graceful step
  Of many a lovely girl.

CLXXIV.

The raising and the rolling bee,
  The feats of skill and strength,
The husking with its noisy glee
  Along the corn-rick's length;
They chose two captains by their votes,
  The captains chose their men,
The winning side sent up their shouts,
  That rung o'er hill and glen.

CLXXV.

They mustered for the shooting-match
  With military air;
With ready eye and quick dispatch
  The rifle rang out clear.
The training-day brought out our force,
  All marshaled in array,
And showed our numbers—man and horse—
  To meet the battle fray.

CLXXVI.

The officers, with belts and swords
  Bespangled o'er with stars,
Who spoke so loud, in short, quick words,
  Seemed bent on bloody wars.
Their yellow tinseled epaulets
  We thought were solid gold,
And men with wooden bayonets
  To us looked wondrous bold.

CLXXVII.

We threw the tomahawk with skill,—
    Could sink it in a tree
At thirty steps, and with it kill
    Or wound an enemy.
As ready as the rifle's shot,
    But not as swift withal;
Nor could we hit the very spot,
    As with the rifle-ball.

CLXXVIII.

We shot the arrow and its dart
    With well-drawn bow and string,
And sometimes struck with practiced art
    The bird upon the wing;
A stealthy weapon in its use,—
    So silent in its flight,—
And when with Indian skill let loose,
    So terrible in might.

CLXXIX.

At nightfall oft we heard the howl
    Of wolves upon the hill;
In numbers they would sometimes prowl,
    And all our lambkins kill;
And when we gathered up the fold
    In yard or sheltered pen,
They sometimes grew so fierce and bold
    They stole them even then.

CLXXX.

And Reynard, that provoking thief,
    Would often rob our roost,

Stealing the hens around their chief,
    Then flying through the frost;
Or snatch the turkey from the coop,
    Fatted for Christmas roast;
But when we chased him,—horse and troop,—
    His life was quickly lost.

CLXXXI.

At first domestic stock was hard
    To get, and hard to keep;
At night we penned them in a yard,—
    The cattle, hogs, and sheep.
The hungry bears would steal a calf,
    Or even kill a cow;
(An army officer and staff
    Once took our breeding sow.)

CLXXXII.

Each child would claim a little pig,
    And each a pretty lamb;
But fathers owned them when grown big,—
    The offspring with the dam.
The boys would claim one half the colts,
    And girls one half the calves,
And many were the stout revolts
    When fathers sold both halves.

CLXXXIII.

When *varmints* trespassed on our corn,
    The rifle you would hear
Around the fields, at eve and morn,
    Guarding the growing ear.
The squirrels and raccoons were worst;
    The deer our wheat would graze,

Until by moonlight we were forced
   To watch his cunning ways.

CLXXXIV.

Squirrels sometimes would emigrate
   O'er fields and rivers broad,
And meet in droves whatever fate
   Befell them on their road;
And well they marked from day to day
   Their desolated path,
Turning from nothing in their way,—
   Not e'en the hunter's wrath.

CLXXXV.

We chased the chipmunk on the rail,
   Swift as a flitting spark,
And traced the groundmole's winding trail
   Concealed within the dark;
And shot the cunning crow at morn
   Standing as sentinel,
To guard the flock while stealing corn,
   And caw the warning peal.

CLXXXVI.

We put up human effigies
   Made of our worn-out clothes,
And o'er the field stretched twine, crosswise,
   To scare away the crows.
If still the cunning rogues would come,
   We frightened them with noise,
Made on horse-fiddle, horn, or drum,—
   That so much pleased the boys.

CLXXXVII.

When aught was left by 'coons and crows,
    And when the corn stood thin,
We sowed our wheat between the rows,
    And brushed or bushed it in.
Oft Spanish-needles grew so thick,
    With each a double horn,
They pierced us to the very quick
    When we were picking corn.

CLXXXVIII.

The meadow-bird our rice would steal;
    And when he was too fine,
He changed his plumage to conceal
    His beauty and design.
Tobacco and the sugar-cane—
    With green and golden leaf—
Rivaled our corn on hill and plain,
    And e'en the wheaten sheaf.

CLXXXIX.

Cotton was pressed in oblong bales
    And tied with hempen ropes,
Molasses caught in cypress pails,
    And sugar bound in hoops.
The rice was gathered, dried, and sacked,
    The paddy nicely hulled,
Tobacco in the hogshead packed
    And to the market rolled.

CXC.

They made a pipe of rough corncob,
    A goose-quill for the stem,

Or formed it of a laurel knob,—
　　An ornamented gem;
And smoked their own tobacco leaf,
　　Or made their own cigars,
As happy as an Indian chief
　　Resting from toils and wars!

VI.

PURSUITS AND AMUSEMENTS.

CXCI.

We hunted on the mountain's brow
    And o'er the prairie wide,
Our home a camp amidst the snow
    Or cave in mountain-side;
And skimmed the lake, so deep and green,
    In boat with oar or sail,
Or skated o'er the icy sheen,
    Swift as the driving gale.

CXCII.

We climbed the highest forest-trees,
    Hid in the boughy blinds,
And felt them rocking in the breeze,—
    The cradle of the winds;
Or scaled the mountain's rugged face,
    High o'er the darksome cave,
Where lightning leaves its burning trace,
    And howling tempests rave.

CXCIII.

We spread the sail at flow or neap,
    Watching the wind and lee,
And brought the monsters of the deep
    From many a distant sea.

The swan could not escape our skiff,
   Nor albatross our aim;
We tore the eagle from the cliff
   In spite of beak or scream.

CXCIV.

The alligator and the shark
   Were oft our wily foes;
For skillful shots the ready mark
   As from the wave they rose.
The one was stupid in his sleep,
   The muddy bay his home;
The other restless as the deep
   In which he loved to roam.

CXCV.

We sought the Indian's hunting-ground
   And rugged precipice,
Where herds of buffalo abound,
   Hard by the deep abyss;
And moving in the grand *surround*,
   First cautiously and slow,
Then springing with a tiger's bound,
   Forced them to leap below.

CXCVI.

The fire swept o'er the mountain's side,
   And prairies wide and vast,
Like sails of flame outstripping tide,
   Or dragon's wings the blast;
Pouring its heat along the plain
   In spite of fence or shield,
Blasting the hoards of grass and grain,
   And wasting camp and field.

CXCVII.

Sometimes it swept away a home,
  'Midst wildest flight and strife,
Consuming buildings—sill and dome—
  And searing human life;
Prefiguring thus earth's final doom,
  As leaping blazes curled,
While human beings to the tomb
  In agony were hurled.

CXCVIII.

Mounted, we dashed across the plain,
  And with the lasso's twirl,
Soon led the wild horse in our train,
  As timid as a girl.
We caught the wolf within the pen,
  And shot the grizzly bear;
We sought the panther in his den,
  And killed the monster there.

CXCIX.

How well we knew the steed we rode!
  He knew his rider, too;
How proudly o'er the plain he trod,
  Or roamed the forest through!
With ready rifle at our side
  We dared the darkest woods,
And swam the river's deepest tide,
  Nor feared the foaming floods.

CC.

We rode with saddle and the rein
  Or halter,—tight or slack,—

Or made a bridle of the mane,
    And strode the naked back.
Familiar with the raft and skiff,
    The scow and the canoe;
Alike at home on wave or cliff,
    On burning sand or snow.

CCI.

The otter and the fisher passed
    Across from stream to stream;
We found their tracks and soon harassed
    And took the furry game.
In the far wilds the beaver lived
    Where slow the waters ran,
His dam and lodge so well contrived
    They seemed as made by man.

CCII.

We traced the bayou's winding course
    Along the fertile lea,
And knew the river from its source
    To lake or gulf or sea.
The waters yielded up their tribes
    In glittering scale and shell;
Tempted, they took the proffered bribes,
    Or felt the rakes of steel.

CCIII.

We sought the fish with torch and gig,
    With bob we caught the eel,
And cut the canebrake pole to rig
    The hook and line with reel.
We baited traps with crab and clam,
    And trolled from shore to shore,

And set a basket 'neath the dam
    To catch the scaly store.

CCIV.

Of leafy brush we made a seine
    Around a long grape-vine,—
Using tough twigs to form a chain
    And leatherwood for twine;
With this we dragged the waters through
    And swept the fish on shore;
The cunning ones—it was so slow—
    Ran under or leaped o'er.

CCV.

To "fire hunt" in the light canoe
    We skimmed the grassy pond,
Or chased the elk and buffalo
    With gallant steed and hound;
Or with our gun, rod, line, and seine,
    Equipments all in store,
We glided o'er the watery lane
    And sought the distant shore.

CCVI.

Sometimes we watched the marshy "lick"
    Where red deer oft abound,—
So near they heard the rifle's click,
    And startled at the sound;
We sometimes scaled the mountain slope,
    Where rocks were roughly piled,
And waited for the antelope,
    So wary and so wild.

CCVII.

We captured bruin where he hid
    In secret "wallows" cool,
And trapped the otter at his "slide"
    As down the bank he stole;
We watched the beaver near his hole
    Beneath the water's edge,
And snatched the wild-cat from his goal
    Within the rocky ledge.

CCVIII.

The early hunters killed their game
    To merely take the skin;
Let none their bold destruction blame,—
    They could not bring it in.
But oft when fat the buck or bear,
    They high the carcass hung;
The settler sought and found it there,
    On the bent sapling swung.

CCIX.

But some, dishonest, sought the wood,
    And lay amongst the logs,
And oft, in search of "wild meat" food,
    Mistook their neighbors' hogs;
When caught their tale was rather lame,
    But oft their heels were fleet;
"Slow venison" was the happy name
    They gave the captured meat.

CCX.

We saw the stealthy rattlesnake,
    With forkèd, flashing tongue,

"Charming" the bird within the brake,
  Hard by her nest and young;
And many thought that snakes at will
  Could charm, with dazzling glare,
Not only birds, but men, until
  They could not break the snare.

CCXI.

We sought the wary sand-hill crane
  O'er the savannas wide;
And cautiously, or all in vain,
  For he would fly or hide.
They sometimes met in flocks immense
  To leave for sunnier climes;
Acres on acres, dark and dense,
  Croaking their noisy chimes.

CCXII.

For water-fowl we went in search
  Near fen or weedy shore,
And pigeons from their wildwood perch
  We took by many a score.
And we decoyed 'neath covered pen
  The turkey,—wild and shy;
He could not find the door again,
  He bore his head so high.

CCXIII.

The smaller boys caught bobolink
  In cage on figure four,
And trapped the muskrat and the mink
  Along the winding shore.
On drizzly days the drabbled quail
  Was driven in the net;

The squirrel running on a rail
    The well-aimed bullet met.

CCXIV.

And sometimes even stouter game
    Fell in their wily snare;
And many a pet was caught to tame
    Which died with all our care.
Ah! how we used to grieve and weep
    When our young pets would die!
We lost our appetite and sleep,
    And sobbed out many a sigh.

CCXV.

The 'coon was oft the favorite,
    Sometimes the spotted deer;
We tamed the eagle and the kite,
    The panther and the bear.
Taught early in the use of arms,
    We knew the art full well;
And trained to labor's cares and charms,
    To think, to act, to feel.

CCXVI.

How proud the boy of his first luck
    In killing larger game!
To slay the stately elk or buck
    Gave him a local fame.
The carcass on a prop was hung,
    The skin stretched on the wall,
The horns above the door were swung,
    Like trophies in a hall.

CCXVII.

No cruel sports were e'er allowed,
    Nothing to pain the sense;
Their strength and prowess were employed
    For justice and defense.
No harmless creatures were abused
    For pleasure or for gain;
None ever sought to be amused
    While others felt the pain.

CCXVIII.

The trapper sought the wild Northwest,
    In snow that never melts,—
Far from the tame, luxurious East,—
    To snatch his furs and pelts.
For half the year the lucky *catch*
    Well paid him for his toil,
Then half the year to watch and fetch
    To mart his furry spoil.

CCXIX.

On snow-shoes oft he trod the snow;
    And on the broadest wave,
In skiff, with oar to guide the prow
    He made the wind his slave;
And in the long and slim canoe
    He darted o'er the bay,
Or up the narrow streamlets' flow
    Threaded the watery way.

CCXX.

Oft out of sight of shrub or tree,
    Amidst the snow and ice,

While earth as far as eye could see
   Seemed locked as in a vise,
He dug the frozen snow away,
   Down to the naked ground,
And there, wrapped in his blanket, lay,
   Resting in sleep profound.

CCXXI.

The Indian trader bore his goods
   Far in the forest wild,
And kept his stores deep in the woods
   Where roved the forest's child;
He held the tribes in due restraint
   By arms at his command;
With blankets, trinkets, bribes, and paint,
   He bought their skins and land.

CCXXII.

The trapper and the trader both
   Worked well for half a year,
And then—as neither one was loth—
   They took six months' good cheer;
Then they would trap and trade again
   Until the season past,
Again live o'er their joy and pain,
   As long as life would last.

CCXXIII.

John Thompson was the red man's match
   In wrestle, fight, or race;
No Indian his lithe form could catch,
   Or follow on his trace.
Ten years he spent amidst the tribe,
   Nor saw a white man's face;

And well he knew and could describe
    Their ways in war or peace.

CCXXIV.

He loved the race, and in the wild,
    Unshackled, loved to roam ;
Nor father, mother, wife, nor child
    Had he to love at home.
He loved to bear the Indian name
    They gave to him,—" White Crane,"—
And left his kindred, friends, and " claim,"
    To seek the tribe again.

CCXXV.

Lud Bailey was Virginia's son,
    Born on the wild frontier,
(His name was Ludwell Washington,)
    He tamed the bear and deer,
And was a hardy wight, I trow,
    So rugged, tough, and bold ;
Barefooted oft he trod the snow,
    All heedless of the cold.

CCXXVI.

And many loved a forest home,—
    A Houston and a Pike,—
And with the red man loved to roam ;
    Some held a deep dislike
Against our brother of the wood,—
    Hating the very name,—
And hunted him to shed his blood,
    As but a higher game.

CCXXVII.

The raftsman with his long, low raft,
    Deep in the river's brink,
Came with the floods; it was a craft
    The breakers could not sink.
The lumberman along the rills,
    With trained and cautious teams,
Brought the best timber from the hills
    Down to the larger streams.

CCXXVIII.

The keel-boat with its running boards,
    The pirogue and bateau,
Crept o'er the streams with freighted hoards,
    Lightened by slim canoe.
When they ascended stream or bay
    As far as craft could go,
A portage o'er a narrow way
    Soon found another flow.

CCXXIX.

The sailor and the son of war
    We have all o'er the world,
To bear our starry flag afar,
    Where'er it is unfurled.
But the keel-boatman with his oar
    And setting-pole is gone;
The world will see his like no more,
    His hardy work is done.

CCXXX.

Mike Fink, Jim Scales, and Hi McClure
    Were noted far and wide,

Last heroes of the pole and oar
  West of Atlantic's tide.
Mike shot a cup of whisky from
  His trusting comrade's head,
Then tried again, and sent him home
  To boat with Charon's dead.

CCXXXI.

Jim Scales was still a surer shot,
  And held in more esteem;
And Hi alone could hold his boat
  Broadside across the stream.
With iron nerve they sometimes tried
  The knock-down and drag-out;
The craven word they never cried,
  And always fairly fought.

CCXXXII.

Sam Jonas and Fred Byerly
  Were noted wags and wits,
From wrong and vice they were not free
  In all their tricks and hits.
But noble, generous, brave Jo Wright,
  With strong and manly arm,
Was quick in danger or a fight
  To save the weak from harm.

CCXXXIII.

Leve Melon was a lusty wight,
  So rough and yet so kind;
Jack Harper was as grand a knight
  As e'er a belt entwined.
Our admirable Crichton—Shaw—
  In everything excelled:

In boxing, boating, logic, law,
   Alike he won the field.

CCXXXIV.

And when we dug our long canals
   Across from lake to stream,—
Alike through rapids, swamps, and falls,—
   'Twas thought the grandest scheme.
Canal-boats seemed like palaces,
   And packets made such speed,
We thought they quite outstripped the breeze,
   And filled man's highest need.

CCXXXV.

Their bugles rang o'er hill and dale,
   And far o'er mountain high,
While echoing rocks sent back the swell,
   Resounding from the sky;
And zephyr bore along the tale,
   Repeating "Home, sweet home,"
Whispered with music's sweetest spell,
   To cabin, cot, and dome.

CCXXXVI.

The keel-boat had a long, straight horn,
   Which oft the boatman blew,
Its thrilling tones afar were borne.
   The skiff, and light canoe,
That shot along their glassy way
   With paddle, pole, or oar,
In silence shunned the wave and spray
   To hug the willowy shore.

CCXXXVII.

We built flat-boats on larger streams,
    And waited for a *fresh*,
Then loaded them with busy teams
    To turn our trade to cash.
Long, deep, and spacious they were made,
    Covered with crowning roof,
And were the only means we had
    To bear our produce off.

CCXXXVIII.

On Mississippi's roily wave
    They sometimes ran aground,
And boatmen found a watery grave
    Where dangers most abound.
Within the *sawyer's* fatal sweep,
    In agony and strife,
A brave one made a daring leap
    And saved his comrade's life.

CCXXXIX.

Some from the city of the gulf,
    Where French and Spaniards dwelt,
Returned as dusky as a Rolfe,
    With treasures in their belt,
Which they had packed through canebrakes thick,
    Where hostile Indians roam,
And o'er the streams, while weak and sick,
    Until secure at home.

CCXL.

At length the stately steamer came
    With grand palatial form,

And swept the waters like a flame,
    In spite of waves or storm.
Yet still the "broad horn" floats along
    Upon the flowing wave,
And still we hear the boatman's song
    And story of the cave!

VII.

HOUSEHOLDS AND INDUSTRY.

CCXLI.

The homesteads stood upon a rise
   Above the lower land,
Or where the "second bottom" lies
   And distant views expand;
And near some water-course, or spring,
   Affording full supply,
Flowing along—a silvery string—
   To where the meadows lie.

CCXLII.

The house and porch, the barn and yard,
   The stacks of hay and wheat;
The field wherein we worked so hard
   Amidst the glimmering heat;
The well-sweep, and the well hard by,
   With pure and crystal flow,
In which we saw another sky,
   As though the well went through.

CCXLIII.

And when we drew the bucket up
   The drops would overflow,
And, falling as we dipped our cup,
   Dimple the waves below.

The simplest and the purest draught,
    The sweetest and the best,
That ever human being quaffed
    From nature's loving breast.

CCXLIV.

The cup was oft a nutty gourd,
    Which, though a little rough,
Served well to dip the gathered hoard
    From bucket, spring, or trough.
We sometimes shaped it like a jug,
    Or bottle with a neck,
Or like a porringer, or mug,
    From which our thirst to slake.

CCXLV.

The corn-crib with its golden ears
    Protruding through the cracks,
Which banished want and all its fears,
    And filled our mealy sacks,
Supported from its wealthy hoards
    Man, quadrupeds, and birds,
And furnished food for kings and lords,
    As well as flocks and herds.

CCXLVI.

The dairy where the faithful dog
    Appeared to sleep so sound,
Yet woe to bullock, horse, or hog
    That trespassed on his ground!
And he would gather all his own
    Wherever they might roam,

    And guard them safely all alone,
      Or bring them to their home.

CCXLVII.

A silvery gray with dappled fleck,
    Of right good blood and fame,
A great white ring around his neck
    From which he took his name.
Stately and large, and yet alert,
    Square head and rounded jole,
With strong, clean legs set well apart,
    And tail a waving scroll.

CCXLVIII.

At morn he followed us to school,
    And watched us come at night,
Or drew us from the watery pool,
    And saved us from—our fright.
If aught befell, how quick he roused
    To see what 'twas about,
And all our quarrels he espoused,
    Ready to fight them out.

CCXLIX.

Whate'er was placed within his care
    He guarded night and day;
If aught was lost, or far or near,
    He quickly led the way.
He'd starve ere he would steal his food,
    Yet knew not human laws,
Or die by fire or field or flood,
    If in his master's cause.

CCL.

To hear his bark of welcome greet
    When one of us came home,
Or when a trusted friend he met,
    You would not think him dumb.
He waked us with his warning growl
    If aught came to invade,
Or with a loud, half-speaking howl,
    He called us to his aid.

CCLI.

Poor Ring! He lived to be so old
    He lost all power of harm,
But though no more so strong and bold,
    He still could growl alarm.
At last came fate's unerring dart,
    And ended his career;
His patient suffering touched the heart,
    His death brought many a tear.

CCLII.

And Tom, the most demure of cats,
    Oft crept amongst the crocks,
Not to steal cream, but kill the rats.
    He climbed up to the box,
Tore the young martins from their nests,
    And dashed them to the ground
With bleeding, palpitating breasts,—
    For that poor Tom was drowned.

CCLIII.

He was a tabby, trim and neat,
    Good tempered and well bred,

Extremely careful with his feet
    Whene'er he went to bed.
In catching mice amongst the corn
    He was a rare adept;
He watched all night, then came at morn
    And crept in where I slept.

CCLIV.

They sought and found him in his bed,
    And tore him from his sleep,
And, all prepared to do the deed,
    They bore him to the deep.
He purred until the noose was fast
    And weight began to swing,
And, unsuspecting to the last,
    Played with the fatal string.

CCLV.

A sudden struggle, and a dash,
    A plunge, and circling flow,
A gurgling bubble o'er the splash,
    And Tom had sunk below.
His golden back and snow-white breast
    Flashed 'neath the silvery wave,
Fainter and fainter, till at last
    Tom rested in the grave.

CCLVI.

I mourned the murder of my cat,
    And sorrowed for my birds,
And long lamented o'er their fate
    With grief that had no words;

I knew not which I loved the most
    When both were wronged and dead,
I only knew that they were lost
    And that my bosom bled.

CCLVII.

How poignant is our boyish grief,
    Whate'er may be the cause!
There seems to us, then, no relief;
    And yet how wise the laws
Which take away the pain and rod
    And leave the love and sigh,
That while we gaze on earth's green sod
    We still may see the sky!

CCLVIII.

The clover-field so fresh and sweet,
    The meadow in the dale,
The growing corn, the heading wheat,
    The grass along the vale,
The frowning, weeping, smiling sky,
    The sun's warm, fitful ray,
Are pictures in the memory
    Which never fade away.

CCLIX.

The buckwheat's fragrance on the breeze,
    The flowers that seemed alive,
The music of the laden bees
    Returning to their hive,
The distant landscape, gold and green,
    The zephyr scarcely lulled,
Charmed all the senses with a scene
    From nature's riches culled.

CCLX.

The garden furnished table wants,
　　The leek and radish-bed,
The lettuce and the cabbage-plants,
　　And currants ripe and red.
The ornamental hollyhock,
　　The peony's gaudy glare,
And staring sunflower seemed to mock
　　The rose that flourished there.

CCLXI.

Soon after winter lost its power,
　　And swept away in floods,
The hyacinth and easter flower
　　Were first to show their buds;
Then johnny-jump-ups next would peep
　　To see if spring had come,
The morning-glories would not creep
　　Till summer brought its bloom.

CCLXII.

We saved our ripest garden-seeds
　　Tied up in little pokes,
Nicely prepared for next year's needs,
　　And kept in sack or box.
In spring they were in great demand
　　Throughout the neighborhood,
To plant and sow the new-cleared land,
　　Redeemed from bog and wood.

CCLXIII.

The beehives sheltered in a row,
　　The bees that go and come,

So quiet when no blossoms grow,
   So busy while they bloom.
And in the working human hive
   No worthless drones remained
To waste their precious time, and live
   On what another gained.

CCLXIV.

We made the hives to hold our bees,
   And gums to save our grain,
And smoke-house, out of hollow trees,
   With roofs to shed the rain.
Sometimes a hollow sycamore
   A man and horse would shield,
Or shelter from a passing shower
   The work-hands of a field.

CCLXV.

The distant hum of industry,
   The busy household din;
The weary stranger passing by,
   Or gladly welcomed in;
Our haunts, the places where we played,
   The bench on which we sat,
And footstool where our mother prayed,
   We never can forget!

CCLXVI.

Our neighbors where we oft had been
   So welcome to the hearth,
Would press us oft to come again,
   So simple in their worth.
Such rosy girls and rugged boys,
   So beautiful and brave,

So hearty in their honest joys,
  Which nothing could deprave!

CCLXVII.

The little girl we loved so well,
  In linsey-woolsey dress,—
Her presence brought a pleasing spell,
  And how her smile could bless!
In all our loves the heart at first
  Is freshest and most pure,
As rosebuds just before they burst
  Are sweeter than the flower!

CCLXVIII.

Yes, Nancy, my young heart was free
  Until it beat for you,
And you were then just ten and three,
  And I but ten and two.
For Margaret next I felt the smart
  That stings the sweetest love;
Eliza won my riper heart,
  But she is now above!

CCLXIX.

Ah! where art thou, my Nancy dear,
  And what has been thy fate?
I never knew, nor could I hear,
  And now it is too late.
But Margaret laughed my boyish tears
  And foolish sighs to shame;
She cured my love, then waited years
  To find another flame.

CCLXX.

Within the meadow, field, and grove
  How faithful and secure
Is unsophisticated love!
  How passionate yet pure!
Young manhood there untainted grows,
  And ripened vigor gains;
Young womanhood—sweet as a rose—
  Its beauty long retains.

CCLXXI.

The lonely shade-tree in the field,
  Its smooth, well-trodden ground,
Where oft beneath the leafy shield
  The ready joke went round;
Where sweet but momentary rest
  Was sought from heat and dust,
And where the four o'clock repast
  Was rapidly discussed.

CCLXXII.

The harvest came in summer heat,
  Ere yet was sere the leaf,
We then with sickle reaped the wheat,
  And bound the golden sheaf;
Then soon we heard the sounds of flail,
  Pulsating like the throbs
Of some great heart, along the vale,
  Dying away in sobs.

CCLXXIII.

We had no patented machines
  To reap and mow our lands,

To do the work of many minds
    And many thousand hands;
And none to thrash and clean the grain,
    No drills the wheat to sow;
Nor had we cultivators then
    The fields to weed and hoe.

CCLXXIV.

The cradle with its whetted blade,
    And fingers made of wood,
Gathered the wheat on field and glade,
    Or wheresoe'er it stood;
But when the storm swept o'er the plain
    And bowed the golden heads,
Then human fingers reaped the grain
    And saved it from the weeds.

CCLXXV.

We thrashed the small grain with our flails
    Upon the hard, smooth ground,
Or trod it out on floors with trails
    Of horses tramping round;
And sometimes fanned it with a sheet,—
    Quite clean enough to 'still;
But when 'twas for ourselves to eat
    We used the fanning-mill.

CCLXXVI.

We went to work at early morn,
    And labored hard until
The welcome sound of dinner-horn
    Announced the mid-day meal;

Then rested one short hour at noon,
  Began again at one,
At four we lunched, then labored on
  Until the day was done.

CCLXXVII.

And when it rained we made our sleds,
  Or boxes for the bees,
Repaired the pitchforks, rakes, and spades,
  Double- and single-trees;
Mended the "gears," cleaned out the stalls,
  Cleared off the thrashing-floor;
If not too busy, got our balls
  And played against the door.

CCLXXVIII.

Sometimes on idle, rainy days
  We crept into the mow,
And read the books we could not praise,
  And did not dare to show.
Sometimes, on Sunday, half dismayed,
  (We own it to our shame,)
We sought some secret place and played
  High-low-jack-and-the-game.

CCLXXIX.

While yet was green the grassy slope
  We had refreshing fare,
From watermelon, cantaloupe,
  And luscious roasting-ear.
When frost had browned the hill and glade
  And dried away the sleet,
New corn our hasty-pudding made,
  And "dodger" rich and sweet.

CCLXXX.

A homely plenty soon we had:
    Green corn and succotash,
New pone, and rye and Indian bread,
    Cashew and golden squash,
Fresh mush-and-milk and honey-comb,
    Warm johnny-cake and jerk,—
All raised, procured, or made at home,
    And earned by honest work.

CCLXXXI.

The cow that cropped the grassy field,
    With breath like fragrant air,
Brought home the golden oily yield
    That she had gathered there.
The bee that sought the flowery brake
    And gained the Hyblæan hoard,
Sweetened for us the well-browned cake
    That smoked upon the board.

CCLXXXII.

With deer and bear, and smaller game,
    (We tamed the fawns and cubs,)
We had our mutton, beef, and ham,
    And pickled pork in tubs;
And sausage, souse, and liver-wurst,
    And loin and chop for broil,
And pure mulled cider for our thirst,
    To brace us for our toil.

CCLXXXIII.

The hunter oft would kill his meat
    When ready for the halt,

And take his bear or venison "straight,"
   With neither bread nor salt.
He struck a fire with flint and steel,
   Or gunlock, by a log,
And while he took his hasty meal
   He shared it with his dog.

CCLXXXIV.

Of sassafras, spicewood, or sage,
   We often made our tea;
Parched rye supplied a beverage,
   Instead of Java's tree.
Wild-cherry bark a tonic proved,
   And made a pleasant draught,
While others stronger "bitters" loved,
   And some too often quaffed.

CCLXXXV.

Oft bonny-clabber, buttermilk,
   Smearcase and Yankee cheese,
The hoecake mixed with white and yolk,
   And sweetened by the bees,
Were added to the hearty feast
   Of palatable food;
Though some might think it not the best,
   'Twas wholesome, fresh, and good.

CCLXXXVI.

We had old-fashioned dinners, too;
   The meat put in the pot,
Then vegetables, fresh and new,
   And dumplings, rolled and cut,
Were dropped in timely one by one,
   And boiled until the feast

Came out at once alike well done,
    All seasoned to our taste.

CCLXXXVII.

The earthen dish and iron spoon,
    The wooden plate and gourd,
Were often ornaments upon
    The rough-hewn frugal board.
Behind the table stood a bench,—
    A puncheon long and wide,—
Set on two blocks of timber staunch,
    That they might there abide.

CCLXXXVIII.

The pewter platter was so wide,
    And basin with its lid,
That, with the plates along the side,
    They half the table hid.
We sometimes hung them in the field
    To scare away the crows;
Whirling, they glittered like a shield
    Brandished to frighten foes.

CCLXXXIX.

We also had wild fruits, which sprung
    Abundant o'er the land;
Rich grapes in purple clusters hung
    And seemed to woo the hand;
And wild bananas or papaws,
    Fresh salads of the soil,
And water-cresses, plums, and haws
    Abounded without toil.

CCXC.

Wild berries were abundant, too,
  Of various native kinds,
Cranberries on the marshes grew,
  Richer than tamarinds.
The service-berry, ripe and red,
  The whortleberry blue,
And strawberries along the mead,
  Most bountifully grew.

CCXCI.

Vines crept below and twined o'erhead,
  For kindly nature there
Her beauties with her bounties spread—
  The grot and wild parterre.
The spring's fresh grass, the summer sheaves,
  The autumn's fruits and flowers,
The shrubs and trees and golden leaves,
  Made their alternate bowers.

CCXCII.

The chestnut-tree with nuts so brown,
  And hickory towering high,
In autumn dropped their treasures down,
  As falling from the sky.
The maple with its precious flow
  In spring-time yielded sweets,
Which, boiled at camp with heated glow,
  Made all our own sweetmeats.

CCXCIII.

When winter broke we made new troughs,
  And set the old ones up;

And made our spiles with bores and grooves
    To guide the trickling drop;
Then waited for a morning freeze,
    And warm, sunshiny day,
To open camp and tap the trees
    And draw the sap away.

CCXCIV.

We often met at sugar camp
    To have our youthful fun:
The fire-light served us as a lamp
    And warmed us as the sun;
And when we went to "sugar off"
    The boys and girls would meet,—
We pulled our taffy in the trough,
    The long-drawn, golden sweet.

CCXCV.

We also found in forest-trees
    The wild, ambrosial comb,
And spite of all the angry bees
    We bore the treasure home;
Sweetened our mead with honey-dew,
    Metheglin, home-made wine,
And added flavor to the brew
    With fragrant root and vine.

CCXCVI.

The apple-tree, the plum, and peach,
    With freighted, drooping limb,
And tempting bunch beyond our reach,
    Invited us to climb.
The trees that bore the rarest fruit
    Were first to feel the frost,

And, like true hearts in life's pursuit,
   Were bruised and broken most!

CCXCVII.

The cider-mill, that creaked so loud
   The neighbors heard the noise,
Oft from the distance brought a crowd
   Of idle, thirsty boys.
The fragrant apples piled around
   In heaps upon the grass,
In winey juice, when they were ground,
   Flowed richly from the press!

CCXCVIII.

From pummace, after it was pressed,
   We made our apple-jack,
Which cheered us at the winter feast
   With many a hearty smack.
Though few the trees along the glade
   That bore the mealy pear,
They sometimes honeyed perry made;
   The quince was still more rare.

CCXCIX.

We boiled the cider—one from four—
   For royal Christmas treat,
And made the apple-sauce—so sour,
   And pumpkin-sauce—so sweet.
And then we made our own sour-crout,
   Put down in tapering tub,
And pickled pig's feet, tail, and snout,—
   A goodly winter job.

CCC.

Our careful mothers bought the tea,
    Spice, coffee, and nutmegs,
And all their little finery,
    With butter, lard, and eggs.
And sometimes laid up money, too,
    Hid in a stocking foot,
And stowed away in some old shoe,
    Or stitched in petticoat.

CCCI.

In spring we laid away our shoes
    And trod the tender grass,
And flew to where the river flows,
    To wade and fish for bass.
We ran throughout the summer heat
    Barefooted, fearless boys;
The stones and stubbles hurt our feet
    And briers quite spoiled our joys.

CCCII.

How sweet at eventide in spring
    To view the distant hill,
And listen while the robins sing
    Hard by the window-sill!
Or in the grove at early morn,—
    Putting away the dew,—
To hear the knavish bluejay's horn,
    And startle the cuckoo!

CCCIII.

And that sweet violet of birds
    That comes with early spring,

With song as sweet as poet's words,
  And heaven upon his wing,
Joined with the gentle wingèd rose,
  In one united voice,
To welcome spring at winter's close,
  And with the flowers rejoice!

CCCIV.

Then soon the swallows filled the barn,
  And martins sought their box;
They pierced the sky and skimmed the tarn,
  In busy, twittering flocks.
The little sparrows, too, would come
  For crumbs about the door,
And sometimes make our house their home,
  And hop about the floor.

CCCV.

The frost in autumn pinched our toes,
  As o'er the field or glade
At morn we sought the roving cows,
  Where they at night had strayed.
We roused them from their smoking beds,
  And, shivering in the sleet,
Stood where they slept among the weeds,
  To warm our aching feet!

CCCVI.

Then soon we husked the golden corn,
  Our feet and fingers bare,
Or gathered nuts at early morn,
  And chased the timorous hare.
A few, more fortunate, had shoes,
  Made by the cobbler's skill;
How proudly then 'midst frost and snows
  They trod the field and hill!

VIII.

SCHOOLS AND COLLEGES.

CCCVII.

In winter-time we went to school,
  In summer labored hard;
We knew the use of every tool
  In shop or field or yard.
And while we thus our knowledge learned
  In plain and simple style,
Our honest bread in sweat was earned,
  And sweetened by the toil!

CCCVIII.

But in the summer, smaller boys,
  That could not work at home,
Were sent, with all their glee and noise,
  To be less troublesome.
And thus the shiny little ones,
  Impatient of control,
Would take their baskets and their pones
  And trudge away to school!

CCCIX.

The old log school-house by the stream,
  Still to our hearts so dear,—
It seems as yesternight's sweet dream
  When we were happy there;

The rocky hill-side where we slid,
　　The path from base to peak,
The clump of bushes where we hid
　　In playing hide-and-seek!

CCCX.

The stream too deep and swift to wade,
　　The waves that would not rest,
But leaped as lambkins when they played,
　　Their backs the foamy crest;
The woods and meadows where we strayed
　　And ran the race so fast,
Are pictures which will never fade
　　While memory's tablets last.

CCCXI.

The school-house had a puncheon floor,
　　So hard to naked feet,
Rough tables and a clapboard door,—
　　A bench the softest seat;
And paper windows greased with lard
　　To let the light come through,
Which thus the winds and rains debarred,
　　And kept away the snow.

CCCXII.

If near, the girls went every day,
　　Sometimes with feet half bare;
The larger boys went far away;
　　But when it was too far,
And they too poor to foot the scores,
　　They to the neighbors went,

And paid their board by doing chores
  Or by a daily stent.

CCCXIII.

The hearty, restless, romping boys
  Frightened the timid girls,
Who fled to seek less noisy joys,
  Shaking their pretty curls.
The bat and ball, the race and ring,
  Were to the boys confined ;
At teeter-board and grapevine swing
  The girls and boys were joined.

CCCXIV.

Fair, tender cheeks, when at our play,
  Perchance were dashed with snow ;
Soon blushes melted it away
  And left their own sweet glow ;
Mayhap the flakes like lilies thrown
  Might fall on some fair breast,
Whose whiteness they could not disown,
  Nor could they be more chaste !

CCCXV.

Then little loves and quarrels came,
  Oft springing from our zeal ;
Here was a coldness, there a flame,
  Perchance some knocks befell.
Our plays were quite severe enough,—
  The wrestle in the ring
Or scuffle,—but they proved our stuff
  In rough-and-tumble fling !

CCCXVI.

If hurt, we never owned the pain,—
    Perchance we muttered *outch !*—
But tried it hip-and-thigh again,
    To see who was "too much."
Such things oft serve to train the heart
    And open forth the mind;
They are of every life a part
    Which manhood leaves behind!

CCCXVII.

Sometimes "the master" joined our plays,
    More skillful than the rest,
Giving encouragement and praise
    To those who played the best.
While thus familiar in our cheer
    We hit him many a thwack,
But still we felt a wholesome fear
    That held our mirth in check!

CCCXVIII.

And sometimes, too, he "boarded round"
    When he was short of pay,
Dividing meals until he found
    How long with each to stay.
'Twas thus he lived and taught and played
    And oiled his wavy curls;
Displayed his learning where he stayed,
    And courted all the girls!

CCCXIX.

At Christmas-time we barred him out,
    A practice not approved;

Nor should it be, as many thought,
    Yet one the *rowdies* loved.
His high command we then defied,
    Demanding holiday;
Sometimes he gracefully complied,
    Sometimes—he went away!

CCCXX.

We rambled round and fired our guns,
    Shot the old year away,
And thoughtlessly interred its bones
    Deep where the centuries lay.
The new year then we hurried in
    With free and hearty cheer,
As if an era could begin
    That would not bring us care!

CCCXXI.

But soon returned the sober hours,
    And teacher's sapient frown,
Whose wisdom taught, with wondrous powers,
    That ten should carry one.
The hazel rod lay on the pegs,
    A terror even there,
Too well acquainted with our legs,
    So tender, red, and bare!

CCCXXII.

We cut and folded thumb-papers
    In shape of boat or bird,
And whispered in each other's ears
    Until the teacher heard;
And then, look out! the pedagogue
    Would show his awful scowl;

With sticks he did but seldom flog,
    But feruled oft with rule!

CCCXXIII.

And other punishments he used,—
    As sitting us with girls;
We thought that we were much abused,
    Yet had our little parles.
And when we made too loud a noise
    By moving bench or feet,
We laid it to the *scrouging* boys
    That sat along the seat.

CCCXXIV.

At home, from Webster's spelling-book
    We learned the alphabet,
And how to spell, amidst the smoke
    And chimney-corner heat.
We then at school learned how to write,
    And some arithmetic,
Then grammar, that we might indite
    And more correctly speak.

CCCXXV.

Of walnut bark we made black ink,
    And purple from the oak,
Or squeezed the juice—as red as pink—
    From berries of the poke.
We ruled our sheets with hammered lead
    In broad and heavy lines,
And there "pothooks and trammels" made,
    With smutches, blots, and signs.

CCCXXVI.

Our copy-books fond mothers saved,
    To show our wondrous skill
In making marks—straight, crooked, waved—
    With pen of gray goose-quill.
We tumbled o'er the leaves so quick
    The pages oft were torn;
Our spelling-book and 'rithmetic
    Were all dog-eared and worn.

CCCXXVII.

When we could spell the hardest words,
    And through the book could read;
We felt ourselves as great as lords
    Who courts and armies lead.
How proud we were to speak our piece,
    Or act the dialogue;
To write our composition nice,
    And play the pedagogue!

CCCXXVIII.

The spelling-school,—I hear it now,
    Though fifty years have sped;
How hard we studied then, and how
    We strove to go up head!
And when the quarter ended, then
    We struggled for a prize;
Than all we ever gained as men,
    Far greater in our eyes.

CCCXXIX.

With spelling-book and Barlow knife
    Arithmetic and slate,

The boy commenced his hopeful life,
    Resolved to serve the State ;
With the Columbian Orator,—
    Which his own hands had earned,—
And Murray's Reader well conned o'er,
    He felt himself quite learned !

CCCXXX.

Smart boys would thus recite their page,
    By blending word with word :
" Father vawl nevry age
    Nevry climer dored
B'saint b'savage and b'sage
    Jovy Jovy Lord !"
Which threw the teacher in a rage
    And all his ire incurred !

CCCXXXI.

Sometimes he let them study loud ;
    At once they all began,
Outdoing Bedlam's crazy crowd
    Or Babel's ancient clan.
While quite impossible to hear
    And difficult to think,
Some Stentor lad would split his ear
    With, " *Master gwout smice smink ?*"

CCXXXII.

Sandford and Merton, Philip Quarll,
    Sinbad the Sailor, and
The tale of Crusoe with his churl,
    Found on the sea-girt land,
Were stories that we all had read
    And faithfully believed ;

And when compelled to yield our creed
   We sorrowfully grieved!

CCCXXXIII.

Our novels were the "Scottish Chiefs,"
   "Thaddeus of Warsaw,"
And "Charlotte Temple," whose sad griefs
   Touched our young hearts with awe.
George Barnwell's story made us sigh,
   And filled our eyes with tears;
Then came the "Pioneers" and "Spy,"
   Which pleased our riper years.

CCCXXXIV.

With Weems's "Life of Marion,"
   "Memoirs of Lafayette,"
And stories of great Washington
   In field and cabinet,
And how the British Pakenham
   Low in the dust was laid,
While Jackson won the hero's palm,—
   The boy high promise made

CCCXXXV.

To be a hero or a sage,
   His country's flag to shield,
And win a place in history's page
   Or laurel on the field;
Or be a famous orator,
   And rise like Harry Clay,
Or rival Patrick Henry's power,
   And win the crown of bay!

CCCXXXVI.

In going to and from the school,
  With book and slate in hand,
How wise we felt to know the rule
  Of three, and understand
Square root and cube! but algebra
  And trigonometry
Were sciences untaught by Ray,
  And not in Woodward's key!

CCCXXXVII.

In higher schools young men would climb
  The hills to *jollygize*,
Young ladies in the summer-time
  Would roam to botanize.
The boys would clamber up by-ways,
  And roll the bounding rocks;
The girls would gather sweet bouquets
  To ornament their locks!

CCCXXXVIII.

Few were the volumes that we owned,
  But such as all commend;
First they were read at home, then loaned
  To neighbor and to friend.
The books, although they ranked not high,
  Were of a useful kind,
And formed our only library
  To aid the opening mind.

CCCXXXIX.

The muse was quite averse to mirth,—
  The Psalms and Watts's hymns

Were much admired, and Wigglesworth,
  They thought, wrote noble rhymes.
A few read Milton's Paradise,—
  The Lost and the Regained,—
More pleased with those redeemed from vice
  Than if they ne'er had sinned!

CCCXL.

Yet there were those who still would read
  Songs of the Cavaliers;
They pitied Charles, who lost his head
  Amid so many tears.
Some loved Rob Burns, and read (aside)
  His " Holy Willie's Prayer,"
And Tam O'Shanter's famous ride
  Across the bridge of Ayr!

CCCXLI.

Few native poets then had sung,
  But Trumbull and Freneau
Were names that o'er the nation rung
  United with Barlow.
And Phillis Wheatley—" colored girl"—
  Was then a mystery;
Her skin was black, her hair would curl,
  Yet she wrote poetry!

CCCXLII.

Newspapers came but once a week,
  We thought with marvelous speed,
Then many came the news to seek,
  And heard while one would read.
The post-boy, who, in muddy plight,
  Rode on from eve till morn,

When coming, whether day or night,
  Blew loud his bright tin horn!

CCCXLIII.

And when to one a letter came,
  'Twas read to all aloud,
It gave the owner quite a fame
  Throughout the neighborhood.
They had no secrets,—all was known,
  Of either good or bad;
For each one knew what all had done
  And what each other had!

CCCXLIV.

To train our minds in mental fence
  We had debating schools,
So strong in native common sense,
  So wise by unknown rules.
And here and there a genius rose,
  Some bright and gentle boy,
Who won the laurel for his brows
  And filled the land with joy!

CCCXLV.

The Declaration, held so dear,
  And Independence-day,
The Revolutionary war,
  And story of the tea;
The tales of bloody Indian fights,
  Of tomahawk and dart;
The Constitution and our Rights,—
  Were known to all by heart!

CCCXLVI.

The story of brave Captain Smith,
    Saved by the Indian maid,
(A pity that it proved a myth!)
    We often heard and read.
And tales of Powhattan and Rolfe,
    Of beef and Johnny Hook,
Boone and the bear, and Putnam's wolf,
    We found in many a book.

CCCXLVII.

And how they bought young English girls,
    And maids from other lands,
With all their beauty, youth, and curls,
    Then won their willing hands.
To dry their tears and hush their grief
    They gave them homes and grounds,
And paid their claimant's golden leaf,—
    One hundred fifty pounds!

CCCXLVIII.

Of Washington, who could not lie
    About the cherry-tree,
They made our daily moral pie
    And Sunday homily.
"In Adam's fall we sinnéd all,"
    John Rogers' piteous look,
How Zaccheus climbed and did not fall,—
    Were in our little book!

CCCXLIX.

The stories that our fathers told,
    The books we knew and read,

Inspired us to be brave and bold;
　The arguments they made
For equal rights and equal laws,
　The songs we heard and sung,
Were for our country and her cause,—
　For right against the wrong!

CCCL.

No right of primogeniture
　(Or *wrong*, it should be called)
Made ten an equal right abjure
　That one might be installed.
Unequal laws cannot be made
　Where equal rights prevail,
To build up one and ten degrade,
　And thus the wrong entail!

CCCLI.

They held elections, open, free,
　Where all expressed their voice;
All bowed to the majority,
　And all obeyed the choice.
The people ruled, and not a part:
　The many, not the few;
The universal mind and heart
　Were honest, strong, and true!

CCCLII.

Sometimes their politics cut sharp
　And separated friends;
Such animosities will warp,
　Though all may seek right ends.
'Twas but a little while they raged;
　"The era of good will"

Returned, and all their hearts engaged
  To serve the right with zeal.

CCCLIII.

The good were not above the law,
  The bad were made to bow,
The strong before it stood in awe,
  The weak were not below.
Each rose or fell by what he did,
  Each gained what he deserved,
Each lost whate'er was not his meed,
  For justice never swerved!

CCCLIV.

The hatred of oppression's might
  Was aimed at every wrong,
While love of justice, truth, and right
  Was manly, firm, and strong.
The hope in labor, study, brain,
  And soul was broad and sure;
While faith in God, our fellow-man,
  And heaven, was high and pure!

CCCLV.

All paths that led to excellence
  Were open unto all,
No class to take the precedence,
  And none condemned to fall.
Official place to all was free,
  Gained by the excellent;
The poorest boy perchance might be
  Some day the President!

CCCLVI.

While colleges led wiser minds
    To learning's higher haunts,
Our common schools, free as the winds,
    Supplied our humbler wants,—
Light-houses on the seas of thought,
    That saved us from the strand,
While lesser lamps in every cot
    Enlightened all the land!

CCCLVII.

The pulpit, theatre, and press,
    The rostrum and the stump,
Were found within the wilderness
    Near sound of huntsman's trump.
The preacher, printer, actor, clown,
    There lifted up their voice;
All went to see and hear, or none,
    As suited best their choice.

CCCLVIII.

The nation was but one wide school,
    Teaching from youth to age,
The continent one mighty whole,
    Its plains and fields a stage.
High aspirations warmed the heart
    On noble actions bent,
Inspired by valor's bolder part,
    And soothed by sweet content!

IX.

CHURCHES AND MINISTERS.

CCCLIX.

At first resound of axeman's stroke,
    The brave divine obeyed
The precept which the Saviour spoke:
    "Go, preach the tidings glad."
And the first pulpit was a stump
    'Neath some umbrageous shade;
It bore the preacher's zealous thump,—
    His method to persuade.

CCCLX.

The tree-tops were their early domes,
    'Neath which they bowed to God;
But soon they worshiped in their homes,
    Transformed to God's abode.
And ere the fertile fields were cleared
    Amidst the forest wild,
The log-built meeting-house appeared
    To guide the wayward child!

CCCLXI.

The little church stood on the hill,
    Hard by the spreading thorn,—
Throughout the week so lone and still,
    So crowded Sunday morn.

The preacher, with his solemn face,
  (Oh, how we feared it then!)
Instructing us how Christian grace
  Redeemed poor fallen men!

CCCLXII.

There sat the fathers of the land,
  Dressed in their homespun neat,
And mothers with their little band
  Of children—fresh and sweet;
The country beau so over-dressed,
  Uneasy in his coat,
And belle by furbelows oppressed
  Until she seemed to float!

CCCLXIII.

Outside stood carriage with a top
  To roll up or let fall;
It went to market, church, or shop,—
  Well named the carryall.
And horses, hitched to fence or limb,
  Perchance with ill-timed neigh
Disturbed the people in the hymn
  Or when they kneeled to pray!

CCCLXIV.

To ministers God's light was given
  For man's immortal need,
Each taught the only road to heaven,
  And each believed his creed.
If in their theologic might
  Their teachings were severe,

They were in aspirations right,
    And in their souls sincere!

CCCLXV.

They guarded well their own belief,
    Baptized the girls and boys,
Soothed us in sickness and in grief,
    And chastened all our joys.
Each labored for his special charge:
    His church, its faith and weal;
And if his learning was not large,
    He made it up in zeal!

CCCLXVI.

The Mormon saint, and Millerite,
    Claimed inspiration, too,
And Revelation of a Light
    That came from Heaven anew.
And various sects promulged their faith
    To cure our ills below,
To take away the sting of death,
    And shun eternal woe!

CCCLXVII.

They told us of the world to come,
    But knew not much of this,
And promised us a heavenly home
    Of happiness and bliss.
If Noah's flood had come once more
    They would have been devout,
Closed up the house and locked the door
    To keep the waters out!

CCCLXVIII.

They seldom thought of worldly means
    To save from worldly care,
But, like the pious saint who leans
    On God through faith and prayer,
They asked of Him to be their shield,
    And to be clothed and fed;
Yet, like the lilies of the field,
    They took no care nor heed!

CCCLXIX.

The State had no established church
    To teach us how to pray,
It left the sinner in the lurch,
    But free to find his way.
'Twas thought that God's eternal laws
    Could govern us right well,
Without a legislative clause
    To save our souls from hell!

CCCLXX.

The hope that springs within the breast,
    Eternal as the soul,
Without a bishop, king, or priest
    Its spirit to control;
That quenchless and immortal ray
    Inspired by Deity,
Which death can never take away,
    Declares we shall not die!

CCCLXXI.

But, taught to pray and fight and preach,
    They thought the means of grace

Were freely placed within the reach
 Of all the human race.
Hoping to win the crown by works
 Performed through righteous faith,
They fought the devil and his quirks
 To save the soul from death!

CCCLXXII.

With tones resounding o'er the dale
 They sung their hymns by rote,
They cared not for the pitch nor scale,
 But knew each patent note.
Nature endowed them with a voice,
 And they could sweetly sing
The psalms and anthems of their choice,
 Until the hills would ring!

CCCLXXIII.

A teacher came who knew each note
 Without its patent head;
He pitched the tone upon a flute,
 Beat time, and took the lead.
On the bass-viol, too, he played,—
 How they did stare and gape!
They liked the sound, but thought it had
 A monstrous wicked shape!

CCCLXXIV.

The biggest fiddle e'er they saw,—
 'Twas more than three feet long,—
To have so small and short a bow,
 And sound so loud and strong.
Some quite admired its rich, deep chime
 In chorus, dance, or song,

But thought to play a sacred hymn
  Within the church was wrong!

CCCLXXV.

They held camp-meetings in the woods,
  Where sinners came to flout,
And heard till they experienced God's
  Free grace, then stayed to shout.
Yet round the camp unchastened youth
  Made most unholy love,
Backsliders, too, forgot the truth
  Once given them from above!

CCCLXXVI.

And big John Smith—the wicked wag—
  Made free with holy things:
He said the story was a "swag,"
  That angels had no wings;
And did not think that Adam ate
  The apple from the tree,
And could not see how Eve got fat
  On such thin luxury!

CCCLXXVII.

He shocked us with profanity,
  And filled us with distress;
Some thought it was insanity,
  Some said 'twas wickedness;
And yet he was a kindly man,
  Beloved by all the boys,
And children to him always ran
  To get sweetmeats and toys.

CCCLXXVIII.

The church rang out its silvery bell
    Along the vale to all,
To call with sad or merry peal
    To wedding or to pall;
And many a couple there were wed,
    In love and honor blest,
And many a grave there hides the dead,—
    The loved ones of the past!

CCCLXXIX.

Ah! there was one, a lonely grave,
    Marked by a wooden post;
No stone was there, no tree to wave,
    And now the place is lost.
Although the dust is blown like chaff,
    Yet God will make it whole;
He needs no mark or epitaph
    To find where rests a soul!

X.

MILLS AND DISTILLERIES.

CCCLXXX.

In early times they had no mill
  To yield its useful aid,
Till they obtained the tools and skill
  And the rude hand-mill made.
They cracked their corn for hominy,
  And pounded it for samp,
Grated the meal and parched the rye,
  To cheer the tent or camp!

CCCLXXXI.

They made a grater of old tin,
  Like an inverted scoop,
And sifter out of half-dressed skin
  Stretched o'er a wooden hoop.
The tin was punched with nail or awl
  And fastened to a board;
The skin was pierced with many a hole
  To bolt the mealy hoard!

CCCLXXXII.

The tedious hand-mill soon gave place
  To cumbrous tread-wheel power,
Which, with its rough, unsteady pace,
  Ground out the meal and flour.

This yielded next to water-mill,
   Built on the flowing creek,
Which turned the wasteful, tireless wheel
   Beneath its sharpened peak.

CCCLXXXIII.

It stood upon a rocky stream,
   Hard by the dam and pond ;
The rosy sunset cast its gleam
   Upon the hill beyond.
As we approached we heard the sound
   And felt its jarring force ;
The sacks of grain we wanted ground
   Were packed upon a horse.

CCCLXXXIV.

We made pack-saddles of the forks
   Of limbs and rough split boards,—
Which often sadly left their marks,—
   And lashed them on with cords
Twisted of bark, and tied below
   The sack to firmly bind ;
Sometimes we rode upon them, too,
   But often rode behind !

CCCLXXXV.

Sometimes the landless laboring man
   To mill would bear his corn
Upon his shoulders, bowed with pain,
   Weary and overborne ;
But, ah ! how sweet the johnny-cake
   Made from its scanty hoard,
To feed his children and to make,
   Though poor, a cheerful board !

CCCLXXXVI.

The inside wheels that turned the burrs
    Were wonderful to us;
The trundle-heads and wallowers,
    Their whiz and whir and buzz,
The strong main-wheel that moved so slow,
    The whirling shaft and band,—
All driven by the water's flow,—
    We could not understand!

CCCLXXXVII.

The miller was a kindly man,
    And bore the sacks within,—
One for the flour and one for bran,
    Then tolled and ground the grain.
Each customer, compelled to wait
    Until his turn had come,
Gladly pursued his careful gait
    Returning to his home!

CCCLXXXVIII.

He had a pair of wooden scales
    Whereon he weighed the sacks,
Thus honestly to make his sales,
    Or fairly take his tax.
He put the sacks upon one scale,
    And on the other weights
Until they poised, then marked the tale
    Upon the doors for slates!

CCCLXXXIX.

The largest weight was fifty-six,
    The smaller ones were halved,

The least were made of stones and bricks,
    To nicely mark the draft.
The people oft amused themselves,
    While waiting for their grists,
By lifting weights on sticks or helves,
    Or on their naked wrists!

CCCXC.

And then they told the standing joke:
    How Hadley yoked his cow,
And how, while he bore half the yoke,
    She pulled him in the slough;
And all about the stone and meal
    To make the balance true,
And how the miller would not steal
    To feed his neighbor's sow!

CCCXCI.

But how he always had fat hogs
    Not one could ever tell,
Nor how he kept them on the bogs
    And made them look so well.
And oftentimes the miller joined
    To swell the ready laugh,
And always seemed to be inclined
    To share the gurgling quaff!

CCCXCII.

The settlement was fortunate
    That lay hard by a mill,
Or near a stream with good mill-seat
    Fixed in the rock or hill;
And it was thought a farm that chanced
    To have a spring or rill

To serve a still was much enhanced,
    And more if near a mill.

CCCXCIII.

Saw-mills were built on rocky streams
    That run by thunder-showers,
With flutter wheels, preceding steam's
    More complicated powers.
They hewed the larger sills and beams,
    The post, the plate, and joist ;
With whipsaws ripped the longer seams
    And pieces to be spliced.

CCCXCIV.

At first they split the puncheons out
    To lay the cabin floor,
And planed them smooth, still thick and stout,
    To make their furniture.
They rived the thinner boards for roofs,
    And longer strips for lath,
And halved the logs for double troughs
    To catch the rainy bath.

CCCXCV.

The lathe was driven by toe and heel
    To turn the buckeye bowl,
And shape the big and little wheel
    That spun the flax and wool ;
They also turned the posts and rounds
    To make split-bottom chairs,
The butter-prints that marked the pounds,
    And various wooden wares.

CCCXCVI.

Distilleries were built hard by
    The springs and oozy bogs,
To "'still" the surplus corn and rye
    And feed the fatting hogs:
Too oft the scene of idleness,
    Sometimes of broil and strife,
Destroying by their wrong and vice
    The happiness of life.

CCCXCVII.

The old distiller, with his face
    All bloated to a puff,
No longer fitted for the race,
    Wrestle, or fisticuff;
His swollen legs, all blue and black
    With many a bruise and dent,
Beneath his weight, with weakened back,
    Tottered where'er he went.

CCCXCVIII.

And yet another one I knew,
    With honest heart and brain;
Although he was a "'stiller," too,
    He was a noble man,
Who, while he sat and watched his still,
    Studied divinity,
To learn and teach God's holy will,
    Which leads us to the sky!

CCCXCIX.

Whisky was used almost as food
    By nearly every one:

The bottle on the table stood,
  And was refused to none.
Some drank and had their groggy fun,
  Nor dreamed that it was wrong,
Yet drunkards were but seldom known
  In all the drinking throng.

XI.

ARTISANS AND PROFESSIONS.

CCCC.

All skillful workmen, artisans,
    Ingenious men of tact,
As well as faithful laboring hands,
    Were held in high respect.
A lazy, dull, or shiftless man
    But little friendship had,
Until he found some way or plan
    To earn his honest bread.

CCCCI.

Millwrights were always looked upon
    As most remarkable;
How they could fix their mills to run,
    With such uncommon skill,
Surpassed our uninstructed sense,
    And was beyond our "guess";
Mechanics all won recompense
    For skill and usefulness.

CCCCII.

Stone-masons were a useful class:
    They took the roughest stone
And shaped them in a comely mass,
    And well their work was done.

Our chimneys were ungainly piles,
   With jambs high, broad, and thick;
At length we burnt the glowing kilns,
   And built the flues of brick.

CCCCIII.

The carpenter was hardly known,
   For all were carpenters,
And very well the work was done
   By self-taught laborers.
They managed by the old "scribe rule"
   To put together frames,
And thought they were quite wonderful,
   With unsquared posts and beams.

CCCCIV.

The tanner bought our hides and skins,
   And all our leather made;
He used the bark of oaks and pines,
   And *shoemake* from the glade.
We dressed the buckskins, soft and tough,
   For leggings, gloves, and caps,
And saved the strips—from horn to hoof—
   To make our thongs and straps!

CCCCV.

And dressed the skins of buffaloes,—
   As big as Dido's ox,—
The pelts of elks and "bounding roes,"
   The gray wolf and the fox;
The otter, beaver, bear, and cubs,
   To make our housing, wraps,
And camp-beds, overshoes, and robes,
   And coverings for our laps.

CCCCVI.

For tailors we had little use,
    We thought they dressed too fine;
And how we laughed about their goose
    And story of the nine!
To make a man, as we could show,
    It took nine tailors then,
And something else—you know; but now
    The tailor makes the man!

CCCCVII.

They sometimes cut our garments out,
    And stitched them with a thrum
To be made up; but most were cut,
    As well as made, at home.
Some one could wear them though made wrong,
    So, if they would not fit
The one to whom they did belong,
    The miss was still a hit!

CCCCVIII.

The cobbler came to make our shoes,
    And while he stayed to board,
He talked of Scripture and the Jews,
    And puzzled all who heard.
He traveled round from house to house
    With apron, staff, and kit;
He loved his dram, and would carouse,
    Yet was a man of wit.

CCCCIX.

His strong shoe-thread was spun of flax,
    As soft as silken floss;

Pine tar and resin made his wax,
    That stuck so tight and close.
He beat his leather on the axe,
    And split his pegs by hand,
And drove them home with skillful whacks,
    Through upper, sole, and rand.

CCCCX.

The village had its hatter, too,
    Who bought our furs and pelts,
And young lamb's wool, as white as snow,
    Of which he made his felts,
And thus supplied us with wool hats,
    And *rorams* with their naps,
And castors made of minks and rats,
    Of various styles and shapes.

CCCCXI.

The peddler with his well-filled pack
    Exhibited his store;
He bore it on his weary back
    Around from door to door.
He showed his goods—pins, needles, tape—
    And glibly told his tale,
Protesting that they all were cheap,
    And made the ready sale.

CCCCXII.

The boys would on the road engage
    In looking at his stock,
Then ask him for an iron wedge,
    And get, perchance, a rock;

He then would seize his knotty stick,
    Shoulder his pack again,
And shame us for the naughty trick
    We played a weary man!

CCCCXIII.

The tinker soldered up the pots,
    The leaky cup and pan,
And burnished all the rusty spots
    Till they looked spick-and-span.
He melted down old pewter-ware,
    All glowing in his flue,
Then cast it o'er as bright and fair
    And just as good as new!

CCCCXIV.

The blacksmith was a mighty man,
    A Vulcan in his trade;
He forged the plow, the hoe, and chain,
    The mattock, axe, and spade.
If artisans had little skill,
    And rude the hand and tool,
Their work supplied the public weal,—
    Useful, not beautiful.

CCCCXV.

They used the English blister-steel
    To make their finest blades,
While Waldron scythes, that cut so well,
    Mowed down the meads and glades;
They "slashers" made that cut the stalks
    Of autumn's bending corn,
And clipped the tops for fodder-shocks
    Until the fields were shorn.

CCCCXVI.

Iron was then on horses brought
   In packs across the land,
The tough, rude bars were hammered out,
   And nails were made by hand;
And salt, until Kanawha's wells
   Supplied the country's need,
Was packed afar o'er Indian trails,
   And so was tin and lead.

CCCCXVII.

And Onondaga's famous springs,
   Surrounded by their lakes,—
The once rich home of Indian kings,—
   Sent forth their crystal flakes
Of snowy salt, like savor sweet,
   Or leaven to the meal;
And many a sack on weary feet
   Was borne o'er dale and hill!

CCCCXVIII.

All were ingenious—boy or man—
   And many things could make:
A water-wheel or endless chain,
   A wooden fork or rake.
They were self-made, and did not wait
   By others to be taught;
Invention was their ready trait
   In action and in thought.

CCCCXIX.

We made a violin—bran-new—
   And run a pewter fife,

Split out a drum hoop, shaved it true,
    Then took the wild deer's life
And made a drum-head of his skin,
    Then whittled out with knife
Two drumsticks,—tapering, long, and thin,—
    To sound the rattling strife.

CCCCXX.

The boys made flutes and flageolets
    Of apple-tree and cane,
And played their solos and duets
    In many an artless strain.
They made their fiddles out of gourds,
    And also made guitars,
And tuned the strings to sweet accords
    That pleased untutored ears.

CCCCXXI.

Long ere we ever heard of Pan
    We made the Pandean pipes,
Of joints of elder and of cane,
    Fastened by barken strips;
Not tuned by scientific plan,
    With stops, or keys, or slips,
But by the music that's in man,
    And played by breathing lips!

CCCCXXII.

We stripped the bark from straight, smooth limbs,
    And tuneful whistles made,
Arranged in sizes till their chimes
    Harmoniously played.
A pumpkin trumpet, when a boy,
    So charmed me with its power,

I gave my pennies for the toy
    That withered in an hour!

CCCCXXIII.

We made our baskets and our brooms,
    And turned the wooden bowls,
Repaired the wheels and mended looms,
    And sometimes put half-soles
Upon our shoes; made handles for
    The axes and the hoes,
And harrows out of crotches, or
    Put stocks upon the plows.

CCCCXXIV.

Taught self-reliance as a faith,—
    The safest human creed,—
They wrought through life a solid path
    In spite of every need.
The daughters whom they loved to woo
    Were neither sylphs nor elves,
But soul-and-body women, who
    Relied upon themselves.

CCCCXXV.

The gunsmith was an artisan
    We held in high repute,
For every one, from boy to man,
    Practiced the rifle-shot.
He made or mended all our guns,
    With locks of flint and steel;
And they were very clumsy ones,
    But seldom failed to kill!

CCCCXXVI.

Whene'er their guns flashed in the pan
    They primed and used the wire,
Or picked the flint and tried again
    Whene'er the snap missed fire;
For they were all unused to fail
    In what they undertook;
If danger came they did not quail,
    But met its fiercest look!

CCCCXXVII.

Still the old hunter loves the gun
    That gained his first supplies,
So often saved his life, and won
    His country's liberties.
What though improvements have been made,
    Or even marvels done?
He wonders at the skill displayed,
    But clings to his old gun!

CCCCXXVIII.

But some believed in spells and charms
    That stopped their balls and darts,
While others thought their good firearms
    Too true for such black arts.
Hair-balls were found in animals,
    Bullets that made no holes,
Which were, they thought, shot in their galls
    By witches, spooks, or ghouls!

CCCCXXIX.

And many were the stories told
    Of people bullet-proof,

Of hunters and our soldiers bold
  Whose guns would not "go off";
And how some guns would always kill,
  However they were shot:
No matter what the marksman's skill,
  They hit the destined spot!

CCCCXXX.

The jack-o'-lantern o'er the bog,
  Or meteor in the sky,
Or shining wood on rotten log,
  They thought the Evil Eye!
Yet many doubted that a witch
  Upon the broomstick rode,
Who still believed a forkèd switch
  Could tell where water flowed.

CCCCXXXI.

And many still their grain would sow,
  Or plant their garden "truck,"
Or choose the time to reap or mow,
  Or vegetables pluck,
Or deaden trees, or fences lay,
  Set posts, or trim their vines,
According to some holiday,
  Or by the moon and signs.

CCCCXXXII.

They told how witches rode the gale,
  And *maremaids* on the wave,
And quite eclipsed Calypso's tale—
  Or Kidd's—of rock and cave.
And they believed the doctrine sound,
  That our old earth stood still;

Because, they said, if it turned round
   The waters all would spill.

CCCCXXXIII.

Saturn and Jupiter were themes
   To them of wicked sound,
Nor in the Bible nor the hymns
   Could any such be found.
That they were larger than the earth
   Was held to be absurd,
For, as God brought creation forth,
   'Twas 'gainst His holy word!

CCCCXXXIV.

Some thought that Saturn, Jupiter,
   Mercury, Venus, Mars,
That shone so brightly in the sphere,
   Were only little stars,
Which, since creation's Bible birth,—
   Directed by our Lord,—
Turned with the rest around the earth,
   Which stood upon His word!

CCCCXXXV.

They thought the "globe of earth" was flat,
   And moon that shone so bright
No bigger than a Quaker's hat,
   And only shone at night;
And that the sun, which shines by day
   With all his brilliant light,
Above the earth went on his way,
   Then sunk below in night!

CCCCXXXVI.

Eclipses darkened all the sky,
   And comets wonders wrought,
Startling the people frightfully
   Till they were better taught.
And earthquakes sometimes shook the world
   From subterranean caves;
Great slides of land and trees were hurled,
   And sunk beneath the waves.

CCCCXXXVII.

Old, ugly women cured disease,
   And watched with sickly babes,
Or chased away whate'er would tease
   By ab-ra-cab-ra-dabs.
They frightened fits and broke our shakes,
   And buried fevers low;
But, ah! sometimes they made mistakes
   And buried patients too!

CCCCXXXVIII.

The doctor, with his calomel,
   Jalap, and opium,
And lancet, tried to keep us well
   And save us from the tomb.
He rode o'er hills and far away,
   Across the streams and swamps,
In rain or shine, at night or day,
   Amidst the fogs and damps.

CCCCXXXIX.

Some cured by water, some by steam,
   And some by *urous* view,

And some could even set a limb
  With gimlet and a screw.
Their patients either lived or died,—
  For they would kill or save,—
And if they killed, why, they could hide
  Their errors in the grave!

CCCCXL.

The measles and the whooping-cough
  We all had to endure;
Our mothers made up doctor-stuff
  And safely wrought the cure.
We scarcely felt that we were ill
  With but an ague fit,
And if it was a third-day chill,
  We thought it very light.

CCCCXLI.

Each household had its medicine—
  Lee's anti-bilious pills,
Peruvian bark, and turpentine—
  To cure our sudden ills;
And jalap looked so much like bark
  They oft mistook the dose,
Which with the patient made such work
  In vain he sought repose!

CCCCXLII.

Ginseng, snake-root, elecampane,
  Sweet-flag, or calamus,
Were dug in marsh, on hill, or plain,
  Prepared and kept for use.
Sweet-anise, spignet, sassafras,
  Spicebush, and wintergreen,

Were made into a drink which was
    Supposed to clear the spleen.

CCCCXLIII.

Catnip and sage and motherwort,
    With tansy to give tone,
Would cure a pain and help a hurt,
    And almost set a bone.
Calumba-root and dogwood-bark,
    And pennyroyal, *barm*,
Boneset, and walnut did their work
    As kindly as a charm!

CCCCXLIV.

Each village had its notable,
    Or sage in history;
Its aged man as oracle
    To solve all mystery;
Its Mother Hubbard with her dog
    And fortune-telling skill;
Its bard,—a Bloomfield, or a Hogg,
    A Burns, or Tannahill!

CCCCXLV.

The lawyers were not popular,
    Their clients were but few;
They made things look so dark or fair
    We knew not what was true.
Of magistrates a small supply
    Answered our honest needs,
The 'Squire the marriage-knot could tie
    And write our notes and deeds.

CCCCXLVI.

And yet the nation's greatest men
  Were lawyers—Jefferson,
Adams, and Patrick Henry—when
  The great George Washington
Made law a fact; men who, with words
  And courage firm and true,
And with a million pens and swords,
  Wrote Freedom's code anew!

CCCCXLVII.

And Marshall, Webster, Clay, Calhoun,
  Still bore the law on high,
And, though unlike, each won renown
  The world will not let die;
And since, o'er all the hills and plains,
  The statesman, hero, sage,
With swords in war, in peace with pens,
  Have graven deep the page!

XII.

PROSPERITY AND HOSPITALITY.

CCCCXLVIII.

We loved the rock and shady nook,
    And sought the river's lave,
Wherein we cast our net and hook,
    Or sported in the wave.
The hill was whitened o'er with sheep,
    Where lambkins skipped and played;
The lazy cattle, half asleep,
    Stood 'neath the cooling shade!

CCCCXLIX.

In yards hard by the river-side
    We penned the bleating sheep,
And washed them in the flowing tide
    Where it was swift and deep.
Ah! how they struggled up the bank,
    So frightened by the shock,
With weighty fleeces, long and dank,
    To join the whitened flock!

CCCCL.

The gabbling goose and noisy duck,
    That swam the waters o'er,
We gathered home in pens to pluck
    And save the feathery store;

It made the stately bed,—"the best,"—
　　So downy and so high,
For stranger or for honored guest,
　　And where a prince might lie!

CCCCLI.

We sheared the sheep upon a bench
　　Erected broad and high,—
The victim held within the clench
　　Of half the family;
And picked the geese beneath a shed,
　　With wings all pinioned tight,
And stocking-foot drawn o'er the head,
　　Lest they would flap or bite!

CCCCLII.

Each daughter had her feather-bed,
　　With ruffled pillow-case,
And quilt,—all white and blue and red,—
　　Made up of many a piece;
A few had six bright silver spoons,
　　Side-saddle, and a cow,
As proud as queens upon their thrones,
　　And just as worthy, too!

CCCCLIII.

How readily they cooked a meal,
　　Or managed brush and broom!
How skillfully they used the wheel,
　　The distaff, and the loom!
How well their needle-work was done!—
　　And they embroidered, too,

Made their own floss, and worsted spun,
　　To work the wedding shoe!

CCCCLIV.

Sewing-machines were all unknown,
　　Each stitch required a thought;
'Twas done by fingers then alone,
　　But now by steel 'tis wrought.
And now they work the daintiest frill
　　Or artificial flower,
And thus by scientific skill
　　Mock nature's wondrous power!

CCCCLV.

On washing-days they sought the brook,
　　Perchance the river's tide,
And soon the kettle's curling smoke
　　Rose o'er the green hill-side.
How they did rub and pound and wring,
　　Amidst the steaming suds,
Then brought clear water from the spring
　　And rinsed the reeking duds!

CCCCLVI.

Washing-machines and wringers then,
　　And patent washing-boards,
Were quite unknown to gods and men,
　　And all their help affords,
Save one most curious of them all,—
　　A woman's tender hand,
Which works unwearied at the call
　　Of duty's stern command!

CCCCLVII.

Upon the twigs their clothes were spread,
    Beneath the drying beam,
Or hung on vines high overhead,
    Hard by the babbling stream;
All bodiless amidst the trees,
    In forms so thin and wan,
They beckoned in the midnight breeze,
    Like ghosts alluring on.

CCCCLVIII.

Young ladies at their quiltings met,
    To talk among themselves,
And tell how Cupid spreads his net,
    As cunning as the elves.
The wedding was a time of joy,
    The belles and beaux were there,
For Hymen and the little boy
    Are busy everywhere!

CCCCLIX.

O love! sweet bond of happiness,
    Witnessed by earth and sky,
A joy to purify and bless,
    And bind the willing tie.
In cabin home and sylvan bowers,
    Strength, manliness, and youth,
Entwined, like trees with vines and flowers,
    In beauty, love, and truth!

CCCCLX.

Many were married by a priest,
    And some by judge or 'squire;

There were a few who thought it best
  To seek a sanction higher.
After the marriage-knot was tied,
  Then came the *chiveree*,
And when the groom took home his bride,
  The infair or levee.

CCCCLXI.

How faithful is the country-girl
  As daughter, sister, wife!
Untaught in all the giddy whirl
  Of dissipated life,
She breathes the fresh, untainted air,
  And keeps her native health;
And needs no art to make her fair,
  Nor gold to give her wealth.

CCCCLXII.

The sons had each his own swift steed,
  With saddle, bridle, whip,—
Their outfit given them as their meed
  For matchless horsemanship.
Some had a piece of Congress land,
  Purchased from government,
While others at the home remained;
  A few to college went!

CCCCLXIII.

And some were "squatters" on the lands
  Until by hardy toil
They earned the means by honest hands
  To buy and own the soil.
And others had "pre-emption claims,"
  Which they could hold by law,

Unless some speculator's schemes
   O'erreached them by a flaw.

CCCCLXIV.

Our Presidents were not more proud
   Upon their chargers fleet,
When on to Washington they rode
   To take the honored seat;
Upheld by right and not by awe,
   And by the people called,
The representatives of law
   With dignity installed!

CCCCLXV.

The boys wore out their fathers' clothes,
   For him not good enough;
Re-fitted and preserved from moths,
   Thus thrice they used the stuff;
For when for larger boys too small,
   They were made o'er again
For smaller ones, so on, till all
   Had grown to stalwart men.

CCCCLXVI.

We made rough button-moulds of stone,
   And pewter buttons run;
And whittled toggles out of bone
   To hold our trousers on.
Sometimes our gallowses were sewed
   On tight at both the ends,—
A very inconvenient mode,
   Yet one which strength commends.

CCCCLXVII.

And mothers, grown too large or stout
    To get their dresses on,
Would turn them over, in, and out,
    To fit their daughters' zone.
They cut off here, and stitched on there,
    As girls still larger grew,
And little ones that ran half bare
    Thought all their frocks were new!

CCCCLXVIII.

No one disdained to wear a patch
    (A rent was thought a shame),—
Selected carefully to match
    From well-saved piece of same.
How neatly, too, the girls could darn
    A stocking, sock, or mit
(A hole would make them blush), with yarn
    From which it first was knit!

CCCCLXIX.

What though they wore their garments patched?
    Their hearts were true and whole,
In friendship, love, and honor matched,
    Uniting soul with soul.
They covered strong and active limbs
    Throbbing with native health,
Unblotched by sins, unscarred by crimes,
    Unspoiled by ease or wealth.

CCCCLXX.

Our summer dress was pants and shirt,
    Nothing on feet or head,

While little girls wore but a skirt
    Of coarse tow linen made.
What happy little romps we were,
    Tumbling heels over head,
With glowing cheeks and tangled hair,—
    So merry and so glad!

CCCCLXXI.

The boys ran hatless half the year,
    Save when they went to town;
The ardent sun oft brought the tear,
    And tanned their faces brown.
The little girls took up their frocks
    To keep the sun away,
The larger ones let fall their locks
    To shun the peeping ray!

CCCCLXXII.

In winter, boys who had no shoes
    Made their own moccasins;
Their heads they shielded from the snows
    By home-made caps of skins.
Our little sweethearts clothed their feet
    With stockings over socks,
And with their aprons from the sleet
    Covered their curly locks!

CCCCLXXIII.

A few young men had Sunday suits,
    Fur hat and handkerchief,
And calfskin shoes, or squeaking boots,
    Which made them proud and stiff;
But daughters, when to women grown,
    Were their own milliners,

Made their best dresses, trimmed with down,
  And muffs of native furs!

CCCCLXXIV.

Young men left home to work and earn
  The means to buy their land,
Or went to higher schools to learn
  To think and understand.
Some labored at Kanawha's Spring,
  Or on some public work;
A few would play at "'possuming,"
  Or act the cunning shirk.

CCCCLXXV.

Some to Galena "diggings" went,
  Or gold and silver mine,
And many were the days they spent
  Ere they had aught to coin.
Some struck rich leads and some had wealth,
  Which raised them proud and high;
Some lost their labor and their health,
  And then came back to die!

CCCCLXXVI.

Some, more advanced, taught country schools,
  Though not of highest grade;
And some that had the use of tools
  Were put to learn a trade;
Some went to town to keep a store,
  And those who saved the pence
Acquired the pounds, and, saving more,
  Soon rose to opulence.

CCCCLXXVII.

Some emigrated to the West,—
    A west that now is east;
Some tried the ocean's foamy crest,
    Some joined the soldier's list;
Some studied medicine or law,—
    Attending through a course;
Some preached the gospel's love and awe
    With eloquence and force!

CCCCLXXVIII.

But, ah! how few in after-life
    At their first homes remained!
It was an age of daring strife,—
    For all was to be gained:
Fair fields to win and be explored,
    Fresh wars to fight for rights,
New States to found with peace restored,
    Denied them soft delights.

CCCCLXXIX.

Young men were of Apollo's mould,
    Young women made to bless,
How finely formed remains untold,
    They left us that to guess.
Bright minds and faithful hearts matured,
    In marriage troth were given,—
'Twas love, not lucre, that allured,—
    The grand design of Heaven!

CCCCLXXX.

Indeed, our girls were very queens,—
    So fair and finely grown;

They asked no artificial means,—
  French stays were quite unknown.
(But when I was a little boy
  I made their corset-boards;
To ask young men they were too coy,
  And blushed to speak the words.)

CCCCLXXXI.

Young gentlemen had neat "store clothes,"
  By tailor's measure cut,
While others wore—up to their mouths—
  A jacket or surtout.
Some wore great-coats with many a cape,
  And some the hunting shirt;
Some buckskin breeches—out of shape—
  With *wamus* well begirt.

CCCCLXXXII.

Fashion had no prerogatives,
  Our social life was frank;
All lived industrious, useful lives,
  Enjoying equal rank.
No pedigree, or wealth, or pride,
  Could trample others down;
No immorality could hide
  Beneath a coat or gown!

CCCCLXXXIII.

But few were rich, not one was poor,
  No pauper could be found,
Nor one inhospitable door
  In all the country round.
None practiced falsehood or deceit,
  The promised word was kept;

We never knew a knave or cheat,
    Nor any false adept!

CCCCLXXXIV.

A friend or stranger found a home
    Where'er he wished to live,
And, welcome, stayed beneath the dome
    A day, a year, or five;
And while he chose to there abide
    He had his equal share
At table, bed, and warm fireside,
    And of the home-made wear.

CCCCLXXXV.

None ever asked him why he came,
    Nor when he wished to go,
If but he had an honest name,—
    For none were high nor low.
When 'twas his choice he shared our toil,
    When not, he took his rest;
Or hunting, brought us home the spoil,
    And all joined in the feast.

CCCCLXXXVI.

The chowder-parties and clam-bakes
    Met near the salt sea-shore;
First having filled their fishing smacks
    And brought the chosen store,
They cooked the feast, which wide was spread,
    Enriched from land and main,
To which the fast ones oft would add
    The brandy or champagne!

CCCCLXXXVII.

The barbecue in friendly strife
   Brought out the orator,
The pistol and the bowie-knife
   Had their peculiar power.
The duel was too much in vogue;
   Though neither right nor brave,
It rid the country of the rogue,
   Assassin, and the knave!

CCCCLXXXVIII.

The nation knew another wrong,—
   The curse of slavery;
The slave, while master grew too strong,
   Lost all his bravery.
The slave's abject docility,
   And master's haughty chide,
Gave one a false humility,
   The other too much pride.

CCCCLXXXIX.

The lordly mansion stood alone,
   An hundred huts around;
One owned the many,—blood and bone,—
   And made them till his ground.
The master's viands as they lay
   Made his rich table groan;
The slave had hog and hominy,
   His gumbo and his 'coon.

CCCCXC.

The master's hospitality
   To half the world was known;

The servant's nationality
　　And native rights were gone.
The one like prince or monarch reigned,
　　Free, royal, proud, and brave;
The other, to his labor chained,
　　Was born and died a slave!

CCCCXCI.

We sometimes found the runaway
　　Hid in the bushy wood,
Who—there remaining all the day—
　　At night pursued his road;
Flying away from slavery
　　To where he might be free,
Ready to flee, to fight, to die,
　　Or gain his liberty!

CCCCXCII.

The master claimed his high command,
　　And ruled o'er every class;
The slave—the worker of the land—
　　Was treated as *bagasse*.
Yet none were happier than the blacks,
　　Whatever was their fate;
The race, though scourged with whips and racks,
　　Could never learn to hate!

CCCCXCIII.

They loved their masters, and were true
　　To all their interests,
Obeying all they bid them do,
　　Even their rude requests.
They worked and whistled, preached and prayed,
　　And laughed and wept and sung,

And on the bones and banjo played
   Till all the quarters rung!

CCCCXCIV.

Though dim their hope and hard their lot,
   And deep the dark disgrace,
A Douglas and an Elliot
   Have lifted up their race.
Far better, since we all are free,
   Though none may be so grand,
That equal rights and liberty
   Should rule our happy land!

XIII.

TOWN AND COUNTRY.

CCCCXCV.

We went to see the wondrous town,—
    Nine hundred people there,
All busy going up and down,
    Oh, how it made us stare!
We heard of cities by the sea,
    And cities on the plain,
And vowed to go, though far away,
    When we were grown to men!

CCCCXCVI.

The rumbling stage-coach took the lead,
    Daring the precipice,
And on safe roads increased its speed
    Until the wheels would hiss.
The driver oft his leaders lashed,—
    So ready, lithe, and quick,—
They trod the corduroy and dashed
    Through marshes deep and thick.

CCCCXCVII.

The weary horseman picked his way
    Through mud and over stone,
With covered hat for rainy day
    And green baize leggings on;

Or sherryvallies on his legs,
    And with valise behind,
Or on his seat his saddle-bags,
    He faced the storm and wind.

CCCCXCVIII.

The tavern with its sign so wide—
    The Indian and the buck—
For man and horse did well provide
    Good cheer and promised luck.
Men there, alone, were not too nice
    In what they said or did;
When women came there was no vice
    Which decency forbid.

CCCCXCIX.

The gaudy sign-board hung aloof
    Upon a lofty post,
And when the winds around the roof
    Moaned like a troubled ghost,
'Twould flap and screech as it would wave
    Like flitting fiends released,
That in their fury yell and rave
    And ride the howling blast!

D.

And many other signs were there,—
    We stopped to gaze and read,—
They blazoned forth the goods and ware
    For customers to heed.
Sometimes their promises misled,
    And oft decoyed the boys;

For there they bought their gingerbread,
    Their candies and their toys.

DI.

Some public places were misnamed,—
    They called them "groceries,"—
Where men too oft became inflamed,
    Or idly took their ease;
Places to jabber, joke, and laugh,
    Carouse and run their rigs,
Or play the fiddle, sing, and quaff,
    And dance hornpipes and jigs!

DII.

The retail store, with shelves of goods
    Which from the city came,
Brought o'er the mountains, through the woods,
    Across the plain and stream,
In broad-tread wagon, covered tight,
    And drawn by six-horse team,
With sixty hundred pounds of freight,—
    An El Dorado dream!

DIII.

The wagoner had trained each steed,
    And matched them all in size;
At his command they all obeyed
    As though their strength was his.
He loved his wagon as his home,
    And horses as his life;
That was to him a princely dome,
    And these dear as a wife!

DIV.

With great blind bridles o'er their eyes,
    To frightful objects hide,
And breech-bands on their brawny thighs
    Some dozen inches wide;
And lofty hames with goose-neck curves,
    O'erhung with clanging bells,
To animate their equine nerves
    And charm the rural dells!

DV.

Few goods were bought at store or shop,
    And at the lowest rate;
Exchanges then were made by swap,
    Or barter—this for that.
There was but little money made,
    And that not always good,
· And yet we always plenty had
    Of comfort, clothes, and food!

DVI.

The sharp-shin and shin-plaster were
    Our common currency,
With some uncertain bank paper
    To glad the longing eye;
True silver coin, or coin of gold,
    Were very rare indeed;
They seemed as treasures all untold,
    And quite beyond our need.

DVII.

We had the dollar,—Spanish-milled,—
    French crown, and pistareen,

And various coins, which by the skilled
    Were known, but seldom seen.
The ninepence and the picayune,
    The fourpence, bit, and fip,
And copper cent were better known,
    But hard to get or keep!

DVIII.

Our court-house with its cupola
    Was once the old ox-mill;
They wagoned off the mouldering straw
    And took away the wheel;
And there the learnèd judges sat,
    So sober and severe;
We entered and took off our hat
    That we might see and hear!

DIX.

The sturdy sheriff frowned his awe:
    He kept the square log jail
With iron grates, in which the law
    Put rogue and criminal.
The judges, lawyers, and the clerk,
    The jury, witnesses,
The solemn oath, the law's strong work,
    All left their deep impress!

DX.

At first the court-house was a pen
    Built by the woodman's axe;
A roof of bark kept out the rain,—
    The light came through the cracks.

The officers and people all
  Looked very much the same,
And equal there met great and small,—
  For all the county came.

DXI.

Sometimes they used the old log fort,—
  All scarred with many a fight,—
Which they converted to a court
  Where might was ruled by right;
Where learning, eloquence, and law,
  Instead of bullets, swayed,
And where with love, respect, and awe
  The people all obeyed.

DXII.

And then the show,—the animals,
  The lion and the gnu,
The ponies with their sweeping tails,
  And monkeys in their blue;
In wax the figures of the great,—
  How very wonderful!—
The hero, martyr, king in state,
  With everything but soul!

DXIII.

The circus-riders, strong and lithe,
  Their feats, the loud acclaim;
For weeks we plied our horses with
  Attempts to do the same.
The clown's old jokes, then not so stale,
  Long furnished us with wit;

To those who had not heard the tale
  We, too, could make a hit!

DXIV.

The wonders of the toy-shop, too,
  So rare and strange to us:
The jumping-jack, the wandering Jew,
  The paper cat and mouse.
How much we had to talk about
  When we came home from town:
The things we saw of wondrous note,
  And what was said and done!

DXV.

And when we to the city went,
  We saw the chimney-sweep,
And little boys with labor bent,
  And girls too sad to weep.
The rich displayed their pomp and dress,
  The poor were with them still;
A few stood by in idleness,
  The many bowed to toil!

DXVI.

We saw the steeples, columns, domes,
  And wondered as we gazed;
Such temples, palaces, and homes
  Our simple hearts amazed.
The noisy streets and crowded marts,
  The churches, parks, and lanes,
And rush of carriages and carts,
  Confused our rustic brains!

DXVII.

Yet still we loved our country homes,
    The fields and forests wide,
And cabins more than towering domes,
    With all their lofty pride.
We breathed the fresh and bracing air,
    Free in our limbs and mind,
For health and liberty were there,
    And hearts most true and kind.

DXVIII.

'Twas sweet to hear the watch-dog's bark
    When we came home at night,
And see amidst the woods so dark
    The cabin's twinkling light;
And sweet the sound of tinkling bell
    On drowsy cow or sheep,
And voices that we loved so well
    Aroused from gentle sleep!

DXIX.

And where once stood, hard by the vale,
    The camp or sheltering rock,
Still oft is heard the startling tale
    Of panther, bear, or buck;
Of hair-breadth 'scapes from tooth and claw,
    And clash 'twixt horn and knife,
Or fight with bruin hand to paw,
    And clinch for death or life!

DXX.

How Boone, the prince of pioneers,
    New fields and forests found,

And won from savages and bears
  The "Dark and Bloody Ground."
With heart to dare and eye to scan,
  The earth he proudly trod,
A hero and an honest man,—
  "The noblest work of God!"

DXXI.

And stories of King Philip's war,
  Red-Jacket and his hut,
The cunning Prophet with his scar,
  Tecumseh and Big Foot;
Of Black Hawk and chief Ke-o-kuk—
  The wary and the bold;
Of fire and flood, in camp, on rack,
  To listening ears were told.

DXXII.

The daring of a Dunstan brave,
  The prowess of a Poe,
Of Kenton, who escaped the grave
  And fled in bark canoe;
How human flesh and souls were tried,
  How hunter, warrior, sage,
Burned at the stake, had nobly died,
  Filled many a storied page.

DXXIII.

And here and there still stood a fort
  Where foes had oft engaged;
Erected as the safe resort
  When savage warfare raged.
It was the pioneer's last chance
  When whites with Indians strove;

Each had its story of romance,—
    Of courage, death, and love!

DXXIV.

The old block-house, so firm, still stood,
    With loop-holes, guards, and doors,—
All built of solid oaken wood,—
    To shield their scanty stores,
And shelter in the forest wild
    The wounded and the sick,
And save the mother and her child,
    The aged and the weak.

DXXV.

The Indian sometimes came to beg
    Where once he had been lord,
And near the mournful scenes would lag,
    Yet breathe no sigh nor word.
The tomahawk slept in its rust,
    The scalping-knife was dull,
His father's bones were in the dust,—
    No relic but his skull!

DXXVI.

Now sons of enterprise dwell there
    In peace—a happy life;
But should the tocsin sound for war,
    They're ready for the strife.
Their exercise—the leap and race—
    Gives spirit to the mind,
While emulation adds a grace
    And makes the heart more kind!

DXXVII.

Brave, honest sons who toil and delve,
  Yet true and noble men,
Defended us in war of "twelve,"
  Then turned to peace again.
The contest which in wrong began,
  And cost us sore campaigns,
Was ended by the victory won
  At famous New Orleans!

DXXVIII.

The nation saw another scene
  We never shall forget,—
The people rose as but one man
  To welcome La Fayette;
The brother of our Washington,
  The friend of Freedom's cause,
Who proved himself her noble son,
  And gained the world's applause!

XIV.

THE CONTINENT AND ITS RESOURCES.

DXXIX.

Our continent is half-world-wide,
    Where mountains reach the sky,
Swept by the winds, and by the tide
    Lashed where the oceans lie;
Embracing climates of the North,
    The South, the East, the West;
Kissed by the sun as he comes forth,
    And when he goes to rest!

DXXX.

The last new land of all the earth
    That man will e'er descry,
Unless some new creative birth
    Shall lift it from the sea,—
For man has traced the circling wave,
    And every foot of ground;
There is no spot to make a grave
    His daring has not found!

DXXXI.

Two oceans with their heaving swells
    Bear up their countless sails;

Two mountain chains, like sentinels,
  Protect the fertile vales.
The rough Atlantic on the east,
  And Alleghany's brows;
The calm Pacific on the west,
  And Rocky Mountain snows.

DXXXII.

Two continents are joined as one,
  Binding the land of fire
Fast to the ever-frozen zone
  And iceberg's gleaming spire;
Swept by the winds of every land,
  And washed by shielded seas,
Nursing the gulf within the strand
  Gemmed by the Antilles!

DXXXIII.

Land of the famed Niagara,
  The wonder of the world,
Where floods from many an inland sea
  In the deep gulf are hurled;
Where stands the adamantine ledge
  While maelstroms whirl below,
Where God has placed the mystic pledge,—
  The bright, mysterious bow!

DXXXIV.

Where bridges span the rolling floods,
  High o'er the rugged gorge,
And where the rocky tablet nods
  And trembles from the surge;
Where earth's eternal pillars shake
  As maddened billows rave,

And, dizzy, reeling to the lake,
　　Sink in a peaceful grave!

DXXXV.

Land of the deep Yosemite,
　　Nature's retiring dale,
Whose stream—descending from on high—
　　Spreads like a bridal veil;
Matched by the park of Yellowstone,
　　Where smoking geysers foam,
Pierced by the narrow, deep cañon,
　　The wild deer's guarded home!

DXXXVI.

The land where nature formed the bridge
　　High o'er the silvery stream,
Spanning the vale from ledge to ridge
　　Where leaping waters gleam.
There stood majestic Washington
　　And carved his deathless name,
Which still enkindles, like a sun,
　　Freedom's undying flame!

DXXXVII.

Land of the broad and hidden cave,
　　With shining gems untold,
Where flows the soft perennial wave
　　Over rich beds of gold;
With column, arch, and corridor,
　　The grotto, door, and porch,
The dome, the colonnade, and floor,
　　Lighted by lamp and torch!

DXXXVIII.

Where mines return the heat and light
  The sun has given to earth,
On which it shone so warm and bright
  Since God first gave it birth;
Where springs pour out their oil and fire,
  As man may smite the rock,
And where his wand, at his desire,
  Commands the lightning's shock!

DXXXIX.

Behold the range of bleak Black Hills,—
  Piercing the snowy north,
Whence spring a thousand babbling rills,
  That bring their blessings forth,—
Glittering with silver, gems, and gold,
  From peak, through gulch, to plain,
With treasured millions yet untold
  To bless or ruin man!

DXL.

Land of the dark and dismal swamp,
  Once covert for the slave,
Where alligators watched to champ
  Their victims 'neath the wave;
But now where fields and gardens smile,
  No more the reptiles 'bode,
Cut by canals for many a mile,
  And crossed by many a road!

DXLI.

The land of calms, the land of storms,
  Embracing every zone,

Where nature shows her sweetest charms
    Beneath the cloud or sun.
'Tis winter there and summer here,
    While yonder spring is green;
The seasons travel round the year
    And beautify the scene!

DXLII.

Where all the climates meet and clash,
    And all their beauties blend;
Where icebergs gleam and glaciers crash,
    And showers and dews descend;
Where sturdy oaks and sturdy men,
    With tempests, heat, and cold,
Wrestle and grow on mount, in glen,
    So strong, so brave, and bold!

DXLIII.

And noblest beasts on earth here roam
    O'er forests, hill, and plain;
The wild horse but awaits the groom,
    The bison bows to man.
The grandest birds that sail the air,
    Or range the wave and fen,—
The eagle and the swan so fair,—
    Fill mountain, lake, and glen!

DXLIV.

Land of Alaska's silvery snows,
    Where flows the iceless main;
Land where the golden orange grows,
    Where waves the sugar-cane;
Land of the famous cotton-plant,
    The rice and Indian weed;

Land where the people never want,
　　Where none may pine in need!

DXLV.

Where yet Catawba's bluey grape,
　　From wild, untutored vine,
O'er many a hill shall blush and weep
　　And give the world its wine.
Missouri's broad and fertile scope
　　Shall yield its fruitful crops,
And fair Ohio's gentler slope
　　Pour forth the ruby drops.

DXLVI.

Where bursting pods unfold their spoil,—
　　A fibre soft as down,
Produced by nature's cunning toil,
　　And rich as silk cocoon.
The cloth of gold, and purple rare,
　　By kings may be unfurled;
The fleece and flax a few may wear,
　　But cotton clothes the world!

DXLVII.

Land of the golden sand and rock,
　　Rich in the precious vein;
Land of the corn and wheaten shock,
　　Flowing with milk and wine.
Land of the valley and the plain,
　　Washed by the river's lave;
Land of the sunshine and the rain,
　　Where flowers and forests wave.

DXLVIII.

Where woods, the treasures of the land,
    Have many a noble tree,—
The oak and ash, the walnut grand,
    Rich as mahogany;
The pine, great monarch of the woods,
    The poplar spreading high;
The cedar where the mountain nods,
    Betwixt the cloud and sky!

DXLIX.

The cherry-tree with lofty form
    And top so tempest-tost;
The sycamore that braves the storm,—
    Wailing like troubled ghost;
The buckeye,—though so vile and mean,—
    The harbinger of spring,
The first to make the bottoms green,
    When birds are on the wing!

DL.

Where iron roads—with palace car
    Darting with arrowy flight,
Crossing the mount and plain afar,
    Pausing nor day nor night;
Drawn by the tireless, mettled steed
    Along the glistening rail,
With matchless and resistless speed—
    Unite the sea and vale!

DLI.

Where telegraphs—that belt the earth,
    Outstripping even time,

Piercing the ocean as a firth,
  Leaping from clime to clime,
And, swift as lightning's bolt is hurled,
  Skimming the lake and plain—
Bear chainless thought around the world,
  Flying from brain to brain!

DLII.

Thus, speeding on with wingless form
  O'er continents and seas,
They join the nation's brain and arm
  To wield its destinies;
Flashing its thoughts on nerves of wire
  Which think but never feel,
And driving steeds whose breath is fire,
  And sinews brass and steel!

DLIII.

The land where commerce brings her share
  Of all the goods of earth,
Where climes exchange, or near or far,
  Each giving worth for worth;
Where knowledge, learning, unconfined,
  To all the world is taught;
Where light unfolds to every mind
  The universal thought!

DLIV.

And where machines soft fibres weave,
  Or bend the trees like reeds;
Where engines rocks and mountains cleave
  Till on the passage leads;
Where vessels sail on dauntless wing,
  And send across the wave

The cannon's crash and rifle's sting,
   To show the foe a grave!

DLV.

Where monitors first won the day
   Against such fearful odds,
Recalling by the dread affray
   The battles of the gods;
Where heroes die or win the crown,
   While steel to steel they join,
And gun to gun, till, going down,
   Their muzzles drink the brine!

DLVI.

Or like the gods, through misty shrouds
   They rise above the night,
And fight their battles o'er the clouds
   Beneath Apollo's light;
Or forge the thunderbolts of war
   Which Vulcan once did wield,
And send them blazing through the air
   Till rocks and mountains yield!

DLVII.

If here no proud Parnassian mount
   Yet rises o'er the scene,
Or yet no clear Castalian fount
   Reflects its glittering sheen,
Broad summits rise above the main
   And on each other shine,—
Across the vale that lies between,—
   Lighting the stream and plain!

DLVIII.

Here yet philosophy shall dwell,
    And here the sciences
Shall send to all the earth their weal,
    Joined with the arts of peace.
No force shall rule or sway the mind
    Save what the truth can prove;
No power the heart and soul shall bind
    Save justice, duty, love!

DLIX.

Land of the statesman and divine,
    The hero, poet, sage,
Where Freedom graves upon her shrine
    The grand historic page;
Where wisdom, worth, and strength combine,
    Where every state is free,
While all in blended union join
    To shield our liberty!

DLX.

Where constitutions guard and guide,
    And laws can none degrade;
Where every man stands up with pride
    And none to make afraid;
Where kings and popes no longer rule,
    Nor trample church and state,
Nor dwarf the mind and crush the soul
    With bull and bayonet.

DLXI.

From Mexic's gulf, linked with the lakes
    That bind the East and West,

From Darien to the wintry flakes,
    No enemy shall rest;
From deep Magellan's whirling flow,
    O'er Andes' peaks and plains,
To Arctic's glittering ice and snow,
    No king shall forge his chains!

DLXII.

No tyrant here shall gather spoil,
    No slave shall bend the knee,
And no invader touch the soil
    Defended by the free.
Mankind shall range the equal land,
    And share the equal sky,
Our country's and our God's command,—
    Truth, Justice, Liberty!

XV.

REMINISCENCES AND CONCLUSION.

DLXIII.

We trod the world where it was new,
    Fresh from the Maker's hand;
Unscaled the mountain in the blue,
    Unmarred the forest land.
Such scenes no more will eyes behold,
    A sight all must renounce;
The old must be forever old,
    The new is new but once!

DLXIV.

How oft our minds since life began
    Retrace in memory
The weary road and lengthening chain,
    Perchance to smile or sigh!
Remembering here and there a place
    Where we have happy been,
Recalling fondly some sweet face
    Still pictured in the scene!

DLXV.

How many times our limbs have ached
    With labor's constant wear!
How many times we've slept, and waked
    To trouble, pain, and care!

How many times the heart has thrilled
    With happiness and love!
How many times, as God has willed,
    We've hoped and looked above!

DLXVI.

The skies seem not as bright and blue,
    Nor earth as fresh and green,
Nor friends as kind, nor love as true,
    As they to us have been.
Whatever future years may bring,
    Our happiest days are o'er,
For Time has borne us on his wing
    Till we are young no more!

DLXVII.

Our lives are muffled by the touch
    Of time until they close,
Our weary forms will seek the couch
    Where naught disturbs repose;
The troubled brain will go to rest,
    The body cease to strive,
The heart lie still within the breast,—
    The soul alone survive!

DLXVIII.

From us all future time is hid,
    The present cannot last,
But there is nothing to forbid
    Us gazing on the past;
And if our past has happy been,
    So will our future be,

Thus we may hope each happy scene
  Will reach eternity!

DLXIX.

Yet time, whate'er it takes away,
  Adds something to our life
Which was not ours in boyhood's day,
  So full of restless strife;
And thus, though with the years we lose
  Somewhat of joy and love,
We gain a sure and sweet repose
  Which boyhood knows not of!

DLXX.

How sweet to win the victory
  And gain the crown of life,
By conquering fell adversity
  In brave and manly strife!
To labor and do all we can,
  Howe'er or where'er placed,
And keep our faith in God and man
  Unsullied to the last!

DLXXI.

The sturdy arm feels not its power
  Till danger tries its nerve,
Nor heart its courage till the hour
  When duty bids it serve;
The soul can never know its strength,
  Nor virtue half its worth,
Until they win the boon at length
  And rise above the earth!

DLXXII.

The ardent hope in work begun,
  The joy of earned success,
The rich reward of duty done
  That brings the sweet release,—
These make the heart so true and brave,
  And lift the soul so high,
That over earth, death, and the grave
  They gain the victory!

DLXXIII.

Ah! happy fortune to be born
  On free Columbia's soil,
Though poverty in life's hard morn
  May teach her school of toil;
To feel a fresh and healthful life
  Throbbing in every vein,
Ready to meet the sturdy strife
  That makes the noble man!

DLXXIV.

With limbs and body strong and lithe,
  And nerve that knows no fear;
With dauntless spirits—bland and blithe—
  To give the bosom cheer;
With hearts to feel, and minds to know,
  And souls to soar on high,
And courage that will never bow
  To aught beneath the sky!

DLXXV.

The fragrant zephyrs of the spring,
  The morning's jeweled dew,

The waving tree and fluttering wing,
    Awake the tale anew.
The axeman's stroke and distant bells,
    The song of boy and bird,
Still ring along the hills and dales,
    And in the soul are heard!

DLXXVI.

I played around the cabin home
    Just sixty years ago,
And hoped that many years would come,
    But they have passed me now.
Away how rapidly they flew,
    Yet seemed to come so slow;
But since my years have grown so few
    They fly more swiftly now!

DLXXVII.

What pleasing hopes once clustered round
    That dear old double house,
Within the little valley bound,
    Yet all the world to us!
The rough old cabin has decayed,
    And there in ruin lies;
Its inmates numbered with the dead
    Still live beyond the skies!

DLXXVIII.

How light and fleet our steps were then!
    How slow and heavy now!
For we have grown to aged men
    And 'neath our burdens bow.
And though the earth now seems more dull
    Than in that long ago,

The sky has grown more beautiful,
   And stars look brighter now!

DLXXIX.

Past thoughts will steal back on the mind,
   Lost love still warm the heart,
Dimmed eyes may dry the tears that blind,
   And none may know the smart;
Bosoms may bleed and bleed—and live,
   Yet no one hear their sigh;
And souls may faint, yet long and strive
   To lift their hopes on high!

DLXXX.

And tongues may talk of hopes to come
   Which still the heart holds dear,
And feet may wander by a tomb,
   Yet cheeks betray no tear;
And lips may smile yet speak no words
   To cheer the struggling breast,
Which still its lost affection hoards
   And loves unto the last!

DLXXXI.

All shed their tears, yet few can know
   The when and where we weep;
The drops may on our pillows flow
   While other eyelids sleep.
Our sorest troubles none behold,
   And none can give us aid;
Our greatest griefs remain untold,—
   There are no ears to heed!

DLXXXII.

What bubbles on the wave we are!
    So soon to disappear,—
That rise and gleam one moment fair,
    Then sink into a tear;
What shadows, as o'er earth we pass
    Like dreams across the mind,
Flitting along through time and space,
    Yet leave no trace behind!

DLXXXIII.

But we can see as in a glass
    The faces that we knew,
And though long years and clouds may pass
    They cannot hide the view;
And hear again the words of love
    As coming from the tomb,
For, spite of all hard facts may prove,
    The voices still will come!

DLXXXIV.

Though eyes are blind, the mind can see
    Whatever it has seen;
The Has Been must forever Be,
    Though ages intervene.
Though ears are deaf, the soul can hear
    Whatever faith believes,
For here or there, or far or near,
    The soul forever lives!

DLXXXV.

We feel emotions o'er again,
    Which but a thought can wake,

Through memory's sympathetic chain,
   That only death can break.
Thus all our joys beneath the skies,
   Our hopes in faith and truth,
Are purest in our memories
   And sweetest in our youth!

DLXXXVI.

But sturdy manhood, free and brave,
   And boyhood strong to dare,
Sweet womanhood, true, faithful, grave,
   And girlhood pure and fair,
With honored age and infancy,
   Through life went hand in hand
As—hoping in the bright blue sky—
   They trod the broad green land.

DLXXXVII.

America! These once were yours,
   The hardy, honest past,
But can we say they still are ours?
   And will our freedom last?
Then man to man stood face to face,
   And hated only crimes,
Bowed to his God and loved his race,
   And bravely met the times!

DLXXXVIII.

Still from the past there comes a voice
   Of deeds most nobly done,
And still Columbia's sons rejoice
   In rights most bravely won.
The charge to hold all equal, free,—
   "The many in the one,"—

And bear the flag o'er land and sea,
   Has now become our own.

DLXXXIX.

One hundred years of liberty
   Have crowned heroic might,
While Justice poised her scales on high
   And held aloft the right;
And still the nation leads the way
   With steady onward march,
Binding 'neath Freedom's gentle sway
   The proud triumphal arch!

DXC.

Already has the great reward
   Aroused the human race,
To gain, if need be, by the sword
   The victory of peace.
And when the blade our sires bequeathed
   For right must leave the belt,
Its brightest steel should be unsheathed,
   Its keenest edge be felt!

DXCI.

Behold the chains of slavery
   Broken by Freedom's blow!
Behold the wreath of liberty
   Adorn the freeman's brow!
Then rouse, ye brave, and sally forth,
   Let heroes lead the throng,
One moment free with right is worth
   A million years of wrong!

DXCII.

As generations passed away—
    So noble, brave, and just—
Have kept the pledge for us, to-day,
    So we must keep the trust;
Thus generations yet to come
    Will still bear on the sway,
Till all the world as Freedom's home
    Shall hail America!

NOTES.

STANZA XXVII.

"*Cradled in a sugar trough*" was a common expression among early settlers, and by no means an uncommon fact.

To rock the cradle, spin on the little wheel, and sing to the baby—all at the same time—were regarded as very advantageous accomplishments in a young mother.

STANZA XXXIX.

There was a general prejudice among the pioneers against giving written obligations for the performance of their agreements. To ask them to give a receipt for money paid, or a promissory note for money loaned, would often be taken as an impeachment of their integrity. The same feeling exists yet among many of the old settlers. Deeds or patents for lands, however, always stood an exception to this rule.

STANZA XLII.

Patroon. This is a Dutch word, meaning patron, protector, master, employer, or tutelary saint.

The early Dutch governments of the States of New York and New Jersey granted certain lands—two miles on each side of a navigable river, or four miles on one side, and as "far into the country as the situation of the occupiers would permit, etc."—to certain persons on condition that they would settle on the same with a colony of fifty persons, over fifteen years of age, within four years next after they had given notice to the "Company," or a "Commander of the Council." Such grantees were called *patroons*.

STANZA XLVII.

Squatter: One who settles on lands belonging to the government with the expectation of obtaining the title. The meaning of the word is well understood in America, but it is not confined to this country. In Scotland those who "squat under tenants," as the phrase is, and occupy their huts and kail-yards, are called *squatters*, and, like American squatters, have certain rights sanctioned by the custom of the country.

STANZA LI.

"Through thickets, *grubs*, and bowers."

Grub was a name generally applied in the new country to any shrub, bush, or sapling that was grubbed out in clearing the land, as well before it was grubbed as afterwards.

STANZA LVII.

Flitting, as meaning a family or a number of persons moving from one place to settle in another, is well enough understood in the Southern and Western States.

STANZA LVIII.

Plunder : Goods which attend the person, more particularly such as belong to movers and travelers. The meaning of the word in this sense is, perhaps, confined to the United States.

"Made up the *shackly fix*."

Shackly, meaning loose, shaky, rickety, seems to be purely an Americanism. It is not found in any of the old English dictionaries, but has long been in use in this country.

The use of *fix*, as meaning a condition, difficulty, or dilemma, is mainly confined to America, though it is sometimes used in England, colloquially, in the same sense.

STANZA LXI.

The following extract, besides supporting the stanza in fact, is so characteristic of the American boy in spirit, that it was thought worthy, "when found, to make a note of":

"A PIONEER BABY.

"In September, 1860, the first babe saw the blue Idaho firmament and breathed the crisp mountain atmosphere under circumstances little less primitive than those which attended its Saviour's birth. David Cartwright and wife were the parents who were rendered happy by the little fellow's appearance, and the boy was born under the spreading branches of a pine-tree, which is yet standing near the centre of the village. This specimen nugget soon became the pet—and, it is said, the somewhat demoralized pet—of the rough miners, and, catching their roving disposition, he rambled around the confines of the camp at the rather youthful age of two years with the apparent ease of an Arab. He was called 'Rock,' on account of his wonderful hardness, and often showed his appreciation of the honor conferred upon him. The crowning act of Rock's life, so far as is known, was accomplished just before he discarded his swaddling garments, at the age of two and a half. While on his way to superintend the working of some extensive gulch-diggings one day, he tumbled head-foremost into a well, where the bottom could only be found at a depth of thirty feet. Upon striking, he only found six inches of water, and didn't propose to be worried much by such a fall, so immediately commenced calling for help. It was his sad fate, however, to remain in there six long hours before being discovered, but when men finally came to the rescue, his pent-up wrath knew no bounds. There was no crying about it, but such a volley of invectives upon the heads of neglectful parents never before fell from childish lips. Here is a sample: ' You fink I kin tay in a well all day wifout nuffin' t'eat like a f'og? 'Fy wasn't no better fadder'n mudder'n 'ou I'd do wifout chillen!'"—*Rocky Mountain News.*

STANZA LXV.

Ride and tie. Most persons will readily understand this phrase. When two persons traveling have but one horse, one rides on a mile or two and ties the horse, the other comes on a-foot till he finds the horse, then rides on past his comrade and ties the horse for him, and so on alternately to their journey's end.

STANZA LXIX.

"They *bundled* on the floor."

Bundling: "A man and woman (not husband and wife) lying together in the same bed but with their clothes on." This custom was practiced in the New England States and in Pennsylvania as late as 1780, and perhaps later. It was not regarded as compromising the virtue or good standing of either of the parties in the least, nor did any particular evil result from the practice. See Bartlett's "Dictionary of Americanisms" and the authorities there cited.

STANZA LXXI.

"Or cypress from the bogs."

In several of the Southern States, particularly in Louisiana, the cabins were nearly all built of cypress. Indeed, the old part of the city of New Orleans was almost entirely constructed of cypress timber.

STANZA LXXII.

Notched and saddled: The method by which the corners of log houses were laid up. The top of each log at the end was sloped from the middle each way, these slopes were called the *saddle;* the bottom of each log was *notched* so as to fit the *saddle* of the log below it. In this way each log was so bound that it could not be slipped either way: the *saddle* held it from slipping one way, and the *notch* from slipping the other way. In building the better class of hewed-log houses each notch was scribed and cut exactly to fit the saddle. In common round-log cabins the notch and saddle were cut by the eye.

STANZA LXXIV.

Eave-bearers were logs cut long enough to project about a foot and a half or two feet beyond the walls of the cabin, on the ends of which the *butting-poles* were laid; against the latter the clapboards *butted* to prevent them from slipping down. *Weight-poles* were laid across the clapboards to hold them on, and the *knees* were short pieces of timber, generally split, to keep the weight-poles the proper distance apart. The first *knee* rested against the *butting-pole*, the next against the first *weight-pole*, and so on up to the comb of the roof.

STANZA LXXV.

"The walls were chinked and daubed."

To *chink and daub* was the method of stopping the spaces between the logs of a cabin, by first filling them with split pieces of wood, called *chinkings*, or sometimes with flat stones wedged in diagonally, and then *daubing* the cracks around them with mortar, or rather mud, which was generally made of clay and water. Lime was seldom to be had.

STANZA LXXXIII.

"On which the trammel hung."

The *trammel* was a long iron hook, capable, by a slide, of being made longer or shorter. We also had iron rods of various lengths, with a hook at each end, to regulate the height at which it was desirable to hang the kettle. The crane was thought to be, especially an iron one, a great improvement on the trammel.

STANZA XC.

Cat-and-clay. I cannot find this compound word or phrase in any of the dictionaries, yet it was generally used and well understood. It means split sticks of wood and rolls of clay-mortar worked tough. The sticks somewhat resemble rough barrel-staves, perhaps a little thicker and narrower. To build a wall the rounds of sticks and rolls of clay are laid up alternately and pressed down together, the sides of which are plastered with softer mortar. They make a useful and durable chimney wall.

"With latch-string always out."

The *latch-string*, passing from the latch inside through to the outside, was the means of opening the door. When pulled in the door could not be opened from the outside, hence the string being left out was an invitation for all to come in,—a general offer of hospitality.

STANZA XCVI.

"The bull-frog's *chug* or bellowing roar."

Chug. Whoever has heard a bull-frog jump into the water will recognize *chug* or *k'chug* as expressive of the sound, though I do not know that the word was ever before used. We have the Americanism *cachunk* or *kerchunk*, meaning a heavy, dull, thumping sound; but it gives no true idea of the sound a bull-frog makes in jumping into the water.

STANZA XCVIII.

"He planted corn among the logs."

I have heard my father say that corn, in the years 1789 and 1790, at what is now Marietta, Ohio, was planted and raised among the logs in the deadings before they had time to clear the land, and he would add, "we had plenty of corn to do us."

In the summer-time their cattle grazed in the forest range, and in the winter were fed mainly on the mast and browse of fallen trees.

STANZA C.

"The bar-share-plow first broke the ground."

The bar-share-plow was made of a plate, that formed the base, and a coulter wedged in the beam. The rest was wood. After the "bull-plow" was introduced, the common joke on the old bar-share was, that "it took ten rods and half a day to turn it round."

The iron part of the bull-plow was made by the country blacksmith out of what was called a *plow-mole*, a wrought triangular plate, with a kind of handle to it, which formed the nose of the plow. The wood part of it, or stock, was generally put on by the wagon-maker, but some of the farmers could do it themselves.

Zane's Trace was a blazed road running from Fort Du Quesne (Pittsburg) to Fort Washington (Cincinnati), and surveyed in the latter part of the eighteenth century by Ebenezer Zane, who afterwards founded Zanesville, Ohio.

STANZAS CIII, CIV.

"Shot-pouch and powder-horn."

The powder-horn, which was in use almost from the time gunpowder was discovered until about 1830, has now become quite antiquated. It was made of a cow's horn, by cutting off a little of the tip and boring a hole into the cavity, then putting a bottom in the large end. Sometimes it was very handsomely ornamented and quite expensive.

STANZAS CVI, CXII.

Corduroyed and *corduroy*, as applied to roads, are words well enough understood by Americans. The noun, *corduroy*, means a causeway made by laying logs or poles across a swamp, marsh, or mud-hole, and covering them with earth or gravel. The verb, *corduroyed*, will be readily understood from the noun. The words are derived, doubtless, from *corduroy*, a well-known heavy *ribbed* cotton goods. And *stalled*, in the sense of getting fast in the mire, was well understood and generally used in the Middle, Southern, and Western States.

STANZA CXVI.
" From *frizzen* caught the spark."

Frizzen. This word, meaning that part of a gunlock which the flint strikes, was in general use throughout the Middle, Southern, and Western States, and, I think, in New England, yet I cannot find it in any of the dictionaries. A friend has suggested that it may come from the French verb, *froisser*, to bruise, clash with, collide ; or from the noun, *froissure*, a bruise, clash, collision.

In " Notes and Queries" (Fifth series, vol. i. page 33) I find the following note:

"The earliest example of a flint-lock proper (not a snaphance, which differed slightly from it in the construction of the hammer and cover for the pan) with which I am acquainted, is the small gun in the Tower Armory, No. 79, known as the Birding Piece of King Charles I., when Prince of Wales, and dated on lock and barrel 1614."

From using the phrase, " cover for the pan," in the above note, we might infer that the word *frizzen* is not used in England.

STANZAS CXX, CXXI.

Beasts and birds of prey are more afraid of man than are the animals they prey upon. Man is less dangerous to these than are their natural enemies; besides, for his own interests, he partially protects them from their foes. Hence deer and game birds, even including the wild turkey and prairie-hen, are plentier, for a time, around the first settlements in a new country than they are in the more distant wilds.

STANZA CXXV.
" The riven oak a fragrance yields
As sweet as fruit or flower !"

I think every person being where oak-trees are freshly chopped or split will recognize a peculiar, pleasant, exhilarating, slightly pungent fragrance arising from the green timber.

STANZA CXXVIII.

" The *truck-patch* and the garden smiled."

Truck-patch : A piece of ground set apart for raising vegetables, more particularly for sale. The word is probably derived from *troke*, to traffic or barter in a small way. Burns uses the word *troggin*, from the same root, meaning such miscellaneous goods as peddlers usually sell.

STANZA CXXIX.

" We *niggered* those too large to chop,
Then rolled and *snaked* the heaps."

Large logs were sometimes severed by laying smaller logs and chunks across them, and keeping up a fire at that place until they were burnt off. This process was called " *niggering*," or " *niggering off ;*" perhaps from the black ends of the logs, or, it may be, from the slow and lazy methods of slave labor.

" *Snaking*" a log is to drag it on the ground without anything under it to keep it from the earth.

STANZA CXXXIII.

" The *rope-walk* ran beneath the trees."

The primitive rope-walk consisted of a path on the ground, with no other covering than the trees and the sky. The spinning-machine was nothing more than a broad board pinned to two posts set in the ground, and three wooden spindles passed through it, with their cranks on the opposite side put into a smaller board, so as to turn them all at once and the same way. It was turned by taking hold of the smaller board with both hands. Almost every neighborhood had some one who could spin and twist ropes.

STANZA CXXXIV.

The domestic spinning-wheel is a thing almost wholly of the past. During the prostration of the cotton interest in the late civil war a few made their appearance, here and there, in the Northern States.

STANZA CXXXV.

" And rap them with the ' boy.' "

The "boy," or "wheel-boy," was a piece of turned wood, about half a foot long, with a head at one end, and sometimes one at each end, used for the purpose of turning the " big wheel." Whenever I played their wheels any tricks, the girls would catch me, and with this " boy" rap my fingers severely.

STANZA CXLIV.

"None left their door
For want of scrip or pelf."

"Carry neither purse, nor scrip, nor shoes:" Luke x. 4.

"While with them ever were the poor."

"For ye have the poor always with you:" Matthew xxvi. 11; John xii. 8.

STANZA CL.

The Lombardy poplar and the weeping-willow, during the early settlement of the country, were favorite ornamental trees. They grew very rapidly, and could be seen far and near, at almost every grave, and in every door-yard.

STANZA CLVIII.

"Yet more by blushes they could tell
Which ones were 'sitting up.'"

Sitting up was the usual way of courting in the country. When the lover appeared in the evening, generally on Sunday, he remained with the family till the proper bed-time, when some one, the sweetheart's brother, if she had one, would invite him to remain all night, and offer to show him to his bed. If he declined to go to bed and still remained, his motives were understood; then, if his addresses were acceptable, the other members of the family would one by one quietly retire and leave the lovers alone; if not acceptable, his sweetheart would retire first and leave the lover with the family. In such cases he soon became embarrassed and took his leave.

STANZA CLXVIII.

"The tumbling brand," etc.

The falling of a brand from the fire towards a young lady indicated that she might expect a beau, and the more it *sparked* the more devoted he was supposed to be.

STANZA CLXX.

Turnip lamp. This was made out of the lower half of a turnip, hollowed out to hold the oil, with a stick stuck in it, around which a rag was wrapped to form a wick.

Slut: A candle made by wrapping a rag around a stick and pressing tallow upon it until it adheres.

STANZA CLXXV.

"The training-day brought out our force."

After the war of 1812 nearly all the States adopted a militia system

STANZA CLXXIX.

"At nightfall oft we heard the howl
Of wolves upon the hill."

When I was a boy, the howling of wolves near my father's house in the evening, in the fall of the year, was so common as scarcely to excite remark or interrupt conversation.

STANZA CLXXXI.

"(An army officer and staff
Once took our breeding sow.)"

This is a true incident of the war of 1812. A scouting-party (as I have heard it related by old people) were cut off from their supplies for a number of days; when they arrived at a cabin, where they could get bread and salt, they were so ravenous that they killed the breeding sow in spite of the poor settler's protest.

STANZA CLXXXIII.

"When *varmints* trespassed on our corn."

Varmint. This is an old English word revived as an Americanism. It is doubtless a corruption of the word *vermin*, with the meaning extended so as to include destructive and annoying animals of the smaller kinds, as well as noxious or offensive worms and insects, to which it was originally applied.

Farmers of the present day can form no adequate idea of the depredations committed on the first settlers by the *varmints*. Whole fields of corn were well-nigh taken by crows, squirrels, and raccoons. The crows picked the ears while in the milk, the raccoon pulled down stalk and all as long as the corn was soft, the squirrels preyed upon it at all times.

STANZA CXXXVII.

"And *brushed* or *bushed* it in."

This was done with a small tree-top drawn butt-end foremost. The method was called "*brushing* in," or "*bushing* in."

STANZA CLXXXIX.

"The *paddy* nicely hulled."

Rice in its rough state is called *paddy*.

"And to the market *rolled*."

In Virginia I have heard it told as a joke how the poorer planters would *roll* their hogsheads of tobacco to market instead of hauling it. Whether the statement has any foundation in fact, or is merely a joke, I cannot state.

STANZA CXCV.

"And moving in the grand *surround*."

Surround: The act of surrounding a herd of buffalo with a view of driving them over a precipice. The word is probably merely a contraction of the present participle *surrounding*. Sometimes hundreds of these animals are killed at one *surround*.

STANZA CXCVIII.

"We caught the wolf within the pen."

Where the wolves most frequented, a pen about eight feet long, four feet wide, and three feet high was built of small logs, with a puncheon floor laid in between the logs, and a lid, made of puncheons also, pinned together on battens firmly. The lid was lifted up and set on triggers, which were baited with dead sheep or deer-meat. We visited the pens once a week, and occasionally had a wolf. I remember a very large black one that fought us through the cracks terribly.

STANZA CCV.

"To *fire hunt* in the light canoe."

A method of hunting deer in the night-time; in the woods by carrying a lighted torch, or on water in a canoe, with the light placed on the bow and a blind set up between the light and the hunter. In this way deer may be approached very closely, and even touched, before they will run.

STANZA CCVI.

"Sometimes we watched the marshy *lick*."

A place, generally marshy, where wild deer come to lick the saline particles in the earth. Other graminivorous animals also frequent licks.

STANZA CCVII.

"We captured bruin where he hid
In secret *wallows* cool."

"During the summer heat it (the bear) enters the gloomy swamps, passing much of its time in *wallowing* in the mud like a hog."—*Audubon*. These places were called "*bear wallows*."

"And trapped the otter at his *slide*."

"This species (the American otter) has the singular habit of sliding off the wet, sloping banks into the water, and the trappers take advantage of this habit to catch the animal by placing a steel-trap near the bottom of their sliding-places."—*Audubon*. In that way they made furrows in the soft, sandy banks, as if a log had been dragged into the water. These furrows were called *otter-slides*.

STANZA CCVIII.

The friendly hunters would hang up their choicest wild meat in the woods and tell the settlers where to find it. I have heard many of them say that their meat for several years cost them nothing but the trouble of going after it. There was no market for anything except the skins. At the trading-points they would always bring money, or whatever was wanted in exchange. Many a home has thus been founded by the rifle. I have heard my father tell many anecdotes of packing home young bear-meat and choice venison hams.

STANZA CCXI.

"We sought the wary *sand-hill crane*."

Just before leaving their northern haunts for southern regions, generally about the first of November, sand-hill cranes collect in incredibly large flocks. I have seen literally "acres on acres" of them, "dark and dense." Their croaking, and jumping up and down, and their stately manner present a most singular and interesting appearance.

STANZA CCXII.

"And *pigeons* from their wildwood perch
We took by many a score."

Pigeons roost together so numerously on trees as to bend their lower branches almost to the ground. With a torch they may be taken from their perch in the night-time by hundreds. The light seems to dazzle and stupefy them.

"And we decoyed 'neath covered pen
The turkey,—wild and shy."

Catching wild turkeys by this method would seem quite incredible to any one who never had witnessed the fact. A pen some ten feet square is built of common fence-rails or poles, about three feet high, and covered in the same way, sufficiently tight to confine the turkey. A trench some foot and a half wide and about the same depth, gradually descending at each end, is dug from the outside under and into the pen some four or five feet, which, next to the wall of the pen on the inside, is covered over with small sticks or boards, on which earth is thrown to disguise the bridge thus formed across the trench. The trench and its surroundings, inside and outside of the pen, are then baited with grain—corn or wheat—thrown about on the ground. Fodder or straw scattered around is an additional attraction. The turkeys will follow the trail of the bait along the trench, pushing one another forward in their greed under the bridge and into the pen. When they find themselves caught, they will run around the sides of the pen, passing over the bridge across the trench, sticking their heads out of the cracks, and never think of creeping under it and going out the way by which they came in. I have seen as many as eight taken at one time, frequently from two to six, but very seldom only one.

STANZA CCXIII.

"The squirrel running on a rail
The *well-aimed bullet met.*"

To shoot a squirrel with a rifle while it was running along the top of a zigzag rail-fence was regarded as a good shot. I have seen it done a number of times, and have done it myself.

STANZA CCXVIII.

"For half the year the lucky *catch.*"

Catch was first used as a name to denote the quantity of fish caught, but it is now sometimes applied by trappers and traders to the quantity of furs taken in one season.

STANZA CCXXV.

"Lud Bailey was Virginia's son."

I have met Lud Bailey often, with two or three bears following him. He generally led the largest one by a chain, and let the smaller ones go with entire freedom. Sometimes he would manage them in this way till they were nearly full-grown. I have seen him wrestle with them and endure their terrible hugs and scratches without flinching. Nothing seemed to hurt him. He would go barefooted in the snow when he had shoes and stockings; he would sleep out-of-doors in the frost without covering when he had shelter and a blanket; he would fell his bee-tree and take out the honey without the slightest regard to the stinging of the bees, and he always saved for his bears a large part of the honey, of which they were very fond; and, what was singular, while eating it they became very cross,—much more so than while eating any other food,— probably from its association with the stings they got when they stole it from the bees, which trait had become an instinct of the race.

STANZA CCXXX.

"Mike Fink, Jim Scales, and Hi McClure."

Mike Fink was well known in Western story. *Jim* (James) *Scales* and *Hi* (Hiram) *McClure* were real characters, as described.

STANZA CCXXXIII.

"*Leve Melon* was a lusty wight,
So rough and yet so kind."

Leve (Levi) *Melon* was a popular rough (if that is not too harsh a name for him) whom everybody liked; full of generosity and courage. He seldom had difficulties of his own, but was always ready to fight the battles of his friends, and always had

"A light heart and a thin pair of breeches."

"*Jack Harper* was as grand a knight
As e'er a belt entwined."

Jack (John L.) *Harper* was a very large but graceful man. He was well educated, and told his story or sung his song most charmingly. The "Scottish Chiefs" was then a popular novel, and to my young eyes *Harper* was the very picture of Sir William Wallace. He shot his father-in-law on a hunting excursion, mistaking his gray coat in the bushes for the side of a deer. There were some, however, who suspected that he killed him intentionally, as they had had some difficulty. He was indicted and tried for the alleged crime, but there was not sufficient evidence to convict him.

"Our Admirable Crichton—*Shaw*."

David Shaw was an accomplished man; medium size, with wavy chestnut hair, clear, high forehead, rosy cheeks, soft blue eyes, exquisite mouth, remarkably expressive countenance, and in form a perfect Apollo He seemed to us to comprehend the entire circle of education, the skill of every artisan, and a knowledge of all things. He was also a wonderful athlete, an unapproachable boxer, a most accomplished dancer and as winning as Adonis; indeed, a perfect Admirable Crichton. But there seemed to be a mystery about him. He never spoke of his home, parents, family, or friends; had no money, never seemed to want any. Sometimes he taught school or worked at various things, but seldom paid any attention to collecting his tuition fees or wages. If he was paid it was well; if not, it was the same to him. The bottle became at length his besetting temptation. He sank ultimately so low that he would do the most servile chore for a dram, and at last died in a stable, neglected and alone.

STANZA CCXXXV.

"Their bugles rang o'er hill and dale."

On the first opening of the Ohio Canal the better class of boats had each two buglers, whose only duty was to play on arriving at and on leaving port. The effect to the surrounding country was very pleasing, and "Home, Sweet Home" was one of the favorite duets.

STANZA CCXXXVII.

"And waited for a *fresh*."

Fresh was often used as *freshet*, a rise or overflow of a river or stream of water, from the rains or the melting of snows. *Freshet* is sometimes regarded as an Americanism, but the word was used by Milton, and in the early history of the Colonies, in the same sense as it is now understood. And *fresh* is still used in Scotland, and, I believe, in some parts of England, in the same sense as it is in America.

STANZA CCXXXVIII.

"Within the *sawyer's* fatal sweep."

Sawyer: "A large tree with its roots fastened in the bottom of a river, the top moving up and down with the action of the current."—*Flint.* With their trunks, limbs, and snags, they form a kind of aquatic *chevaux-de-frise*, very dangerous to boats. Sometimes they float careering with the current, or catch in the middle and see-saw, and are still formidable. They abound more in the large rivers, particularly in the Mississippi and Missouri. They are seldom seen in the Ohio.

"A brave one made a daring leap
And saved his comrade's life."

John Westenhaver leaped from the deck of a covered flat-boat to the blade of the oar, and saved the life of *James Cobbum*, who was about to sink and pass under the boat. It was a feat of noble daring, marvelous agility, and strength.

STANZA CCXL.

"Yet still the 'broad horn' floats along."

Broad horn: The name in the Western country for covered flat-boats.

"And story of the cave."

This alludes to a cave in the north bank of the Ohio River, inhabited by outlaws in early times, who used to kill and rob the flat-boat-men. Chas. A. Jones has written a poem on the subject.

STANZAS CCXLVI, CCLVII.

The story of *Ring* is a true tale, and the fate of poor *Tom* no idle fiction.

STANZA CCLXIV.

" Sometimes a hollow sycamore
A man and horse would shield."

The size to which the sycamore-trees sometimes grew was enormous, and when very large they were uniformly hollow. One stood just below my father's house, which had been used for many years as a smoke-house. It had an opening on one side, in which a door was hung, and was so large in the hollow that a man could ride through the door on horseback into the tree, turn round and come out without dismounting. This feat was actually done by a man whose name was *Jesse Loring*. On another part of the farm there was a much larger sycamore. It had shot up three immense trunks to a great height, which, for some twenty feet at the bottom, were united in one round base. The tree had been deadened for many years, and ultimately the separate trunks broke off and fell, leaving the base, as a great stump, standing. One day, as we were at work near the place, my father *boosted* me up on the outside and helped me down on the inside, for the purpose of measuring the diameter of the tree. As high as I could reach up from the ground, we found the space to be twenty-two feet. This, allowing one foot for the thickness of the shell, which was about its thickness, would give a circumference of at least seventy-five feet. Such trees were sometimes used as dwelling-places by the early settlers until they could build their cabins.

The hollow trunks of sycamore-trees, cut into proper sections, were often dressed out to make bins to put in barns, or set up and roofed for the purpose of housing tools. I have often seen my father dressing out these *gums*, which, when lying on the side, would allow him to stand erect in the hollow.

STANZA CCLXXIX.

Dodger: A cake made of Indian corn-meal and baked hard. It is peculiarly sweet when made of new corn. *Dodger*, *hoe-cake*, *pone*, and *johnny-cake* differ very little except in the method of baking. In their plainest state they are simply Indian corn-meal and a little salt, wet up with water and baked. They can be much improved, of course, by other ingredients. The rye and Indian bread was similar to the pone, except that there was a mixture of rye-flour with the corn-meal.

Mush is sometimes called *hasty-pudding*. It is merely Indian corn-meal boiled in water, constantly stirred during the boiling, and salted palatably. *Mush-and-milk* was a favorite dish for supper. *Mush* was also eaten simply with *butter*, or with *honey* or *molasses*.

Succotash scarcely needs a definition in America. There are several derivations of the word, all, perhaps, merely fanciful. It is an Indian word, first heard among the Narragansets, meaning corn boiled whole. It now generally means grains of green corn cut from the cob and green beans boiled together.

Roasting ears: The ears of green corn in that stage of growth suitable for roasting, while they are yet in the *husk*, as it is called; they are very delicious *roasted* before an open fire. The usual mode of cooking them now, however, is by boiling. Yet, as a general name, they are still called *roasting ears*.

STANZA CCLXXXVIII.

Pewter platters, plates, etc.

"We sometimes hung them in the field
To scare away the crows."

This is literally true, and they make a very efficient scarecrow. Hung up by a string in the open air, they will keep constantly in motion by the slightest breeze. My father had holes drilled through the rims of all our large pewter dishes for that purpose. The breeze twists up the string, the weight of the platter untwists it, and thus they are kept constantly glittering in the sun.

STANZA CCCX.

At the foot of the hill on which the school-house stood there was a narrow, swift place in the river called the "Sheep Jump." It was said to have been named from the resemblance of the foam on the crests of the waves, as they tumbled over the rocks, to the backs of sheep as they leap over a fence or bar.

STANZA CCCXVI.

Outch: An exclamation on being slightly, but suddenly or unexpectedly, hurt. I cannot find this word in any of the dictionaries. There is an old Scottish word, *oich*, meaning prostration or fatigue from great muscular exertion, which possibly may be the parent of *outch;* or it may be merely an interjection without etymology or rule. And there is an absolute English provincialism, *ouche*, meaning a clasp or jewel, as a lady's bracelet; but this can scarcely be the same word.

Hip-and-thigh. This compound was much in use many years ago, and perhaps may be yet. In a good-natured sense it is the equivalent of *rough-and-ready.* "And he smote them hip and thigh with a great slaughter." Judges xv. 8.

Too much. This phrase was generally in use, meaning too strong or too powerful. It is similar to another form, and better authorized use, of the word much, as, "he is very *much* of a man," "it is not *much* of a shower," etc.

NOTES.

STANZA CCCXVIII.

Boarded round. The practice of each patron boarding the schoolmaster in proportion to the number of pupils he sent was not uncommon.

I once heard the story of a stingy old patron whose duty to the pedagogue was to board him a certain number of meals and a fraction over. At his last meal the old gentleman reminded the teacher that there was due him only half a meal; "but," said he, "you may eat nearly as much as you want to."

STANZA CCCXIX.

"At Christmas-time we *barred him out.*"

The practice of the pupils barring out the school-master at Christmas prevailed generally throughout the South and West. The teacher would find the school-house barricaded; written propositions would be sent to him to give the insurgents a holiday; so many apples, such a quantity of ginger-bread and cakes, and so much beer or whisky,—an agreement to which was the condition precedent to his entering the school-house. After a suitable show of surprise, dignity, and resistance, he would gracefully grant the terms, and sometimes join the pupils in their merriment. Some teachers, however, more particularly those from the New England States, would take it in "high dudgeon," go off and leave the boys in peaceable possession of the fortress for some days before matters could be accommodated.

STANZA CCCXX.

The practice in the country of going round the neighborhood and firing guns on the evening of the last day in the year, prevailed very generally fifty years ago, but I believe now it is entirely disused.

STANZA CCCXXIII.

"We laid it to the *scrouging* boys."

Scrouging. This word was much used, especially by school-boys, in the same sense as *crowding*, of which I suppose it to be a corruption.

STANZA CCCXXVIII.

"And when the quarter ended, then
We struggled for a prize."

The prize, which was generally a penknife, pocket-book, medal, or something of the kind, was placed near the head of the class, so that the successful pupil, as soon as the question was decided, could reach it at once.

STANZA CCCXXX.

It need hardly be said that the quoted lines in this stanza, if read correctly, would constitute the first verse of the "Universal Prayer," by Pope:

> "Father of all, in every age,
> In every clime adored,
> By saint, by savage, and by sage,
> Jehovah, Jove, or Lord."

STANZA CCCXXXI.

"*Master gwout smice smink?*"

If these compressed words were allowed to expand to their full dimensions they would read as follows:

"*Master, may I go out and get some ice to put in my ink?*"

STANZA CCCXXXVII.

Jollygize: geologize.

STANZA CCCXXXIX.

Michael Wigglesworth was born in England, but came to Massachusetts when a boy. He wrote a long poem entitled "The Day of Doom," which, without any extravagance of language, was lugubriously solemn and horribly awful. He was also the author of many other pieces of prose and poetry, principally on religious subjects.

STANZA CCCXLVII.

"And how they *bought young English girls*."

The early settlers of Virginia bought young girls on their arrival from the Old Country, and gave one hundred and fifty pounds of tobacco (about the weight of the girls) apiece for them, and made them honored wives, who became honored mothers of an honored race.

STANZA CCCXLVIII.

"Were in our *little book*."

The New England Primer. This book is now a rare curiosity.

STANZA CCCLXVII.

"Closed up the house and locked the door
To keep the waters out!"

When I was a lad I often heard the following story told of a divine who had been called to preach at Marietta, Ohio; I think his name was *Trowbridge*. It appeared that he had scarcely ever been outside of a theological seminary, or some religious college, in his life, and consequently knew but little of the world he lived in. Soon after his settlement in Marietta some of his church-members presented him with a barrel of new cider. In a few days, much to his surprise and dismay, he found the hoops broken and the barrel empty. He ran to his neighbors with the astonishing news; but his more worldly-wise friends only smiled, and told him that he should have bored a gimlet-hole in the top of the barrel near the bung, to allow the gases to escape while the cider was fermenting. This was all new information to the parson; but he resolved to thenceforth profit by his newly-gotten and dearly-bought knowledge. So, not long afterwards, his friends presented him with a half-dozen barrels of choice winter apples, carefully headed up. *The parson was very particular to have a gimlet-hole bored in every one of the apple-barrels!*

Another story was told of the same parson: On the occasion of a rise in the waters at the confluence of the Ohio and Muskingum Rivers, when the town was about to be inundated, the parson's neighbors went to look after his interests, and, if necessary, rescue him from danger. They found him in his library composedly reading his Bible, while the flood, which had already invaded his stable to the depth of several feet, was rapidly approaching his house. On his friends expressing some surprise, he, with one hand on his Bible and the other on his heart, assured them that all was well with him. "But," inquired they, hastily, "parson, parson, where is your horse and cow?" "Oh, my dear friends," replied the parson, "be not uneasy about them, they are perfectly safe; *I put them in the stable and locked the door very carefully!*"

STANZA CCCLXXVI.

"And big *John Smith*," etc.

This *John Smith* was not a myth, but a real person, who weighed three hundred and forty pounds!

STANZAS CCCXCVII, CCCXCVIII.

The two distillers mentioned in these stanzas were real characters. The first one need not be named; the name of the second one was *James Manning*. It seems to me that he was afterwards settled as a minister, in or near Athens, Ohio.

STANZA CCCCIV.

Shoemake. The popular name of *sumach*.

STANZA CCCCX.

"And *rorams* with their naps."

Roram. I cannot find this word anywhere, and know nothing of its proper orthography, but it was the well-known name of a kind of hat made of wool or coarse fur, and napped. A hat made of all fur, as every one knows, was called a castor, from the beaver. When both kinds were napped it required some skill to tell one from the other, and from this fact frauds were sometimes practiced by selling *rorams* for *castors.*

STANZA CCCCXII.

This stanza describes a favorite joke practiced on pack-peddlers by mischievous boys; but they did it at their peril, for they were sometimes caught and smartly drubbed for their temerity.

STANZA CCCCXXII.

"*A pumpkin trumpet,*" etc.

On my way to school one morning, I was overtaken by a schoolmate, older than myself, who had a little trumpet made of the stem of a pumpkin-vine. The leaf was trimmed off so as not to perforate the end of the tube, which was slit in such a way—well enough understood by older boys—as when inserted in the mouth and blown through, it gave out a grave, soft, reedy sound. It was a new thing to me. I had three copper cents, which I carried in a little diamond-shaped japanned tin box. I forthwith offered them, box and all, for the trumpet. The offer was accepted and the property delivered. I blew my own trumpet a short time with great delight, but soon coming near the school-house, I hid it in a fence corner. At noon I eagerly ran to get it, but my trumpet had wilted and would sound no more.

This was long before I had heard of Dr. Franklin's "whistle," which, when I first read it, forcibly reminded me of my pumpkin-stem trumpet. Perhaps Dr. Franklin intended his story to "point a moral;" if so, mine has the advantage of it in being strictly true in fact.

STANZA CCCCXXXIX.

"And some could even set a limb
With gimlet and a screw."

I knew an instance—the facts were developed in a lawsuit—where a country doctor, in setting an oblique fracture of a leg bone (*tibia*), laid open the flesh, and bored a gimlet hole through the lapping ends of the bone and fastened them together with a common iron screw.

NOTES.

STANZA CCCCXLIV.
"A Burns, or *Tannahill*."

The *Tannahill* mentioned in this stanza was from Paisley, Scotland, and probably of the same family that gave the world Robert Tannahill, the Scottish poet. *Samuel Tannahill* was a fine specimen of the American pioneer: a hunter, farmer, justice of the peace. He wrote verses on local subjects with great facility, and, like Burns, was a terror to over-pious people.

STANZA CCCCLX.
"Then came the *chiveree*."

Chiveree is a corruption of the French word *charivari*, loud, ludicrous, or burlesque music made on tin pans, kettles, bells, etc. Confused noise, clatter. The practice of *belling* young married people, as it is sometimes called, is not entirely disused yet.

STANZA CCCCLXIV.
"Our Presidents were not more proud."

Thomas Jefferson rode to Washington on horseback to be inaugurated President of the United States. *Andrew Jackson* walked from the White House to the Capitol to take the oath of office.

STANZA CCCCLXXIV.
"A few would play at 'possuming."

"In the common parlance of the country, any one who counterfeits sickness, or dissembles strongly for a particular purpose, is said to be '*possuming*.'"—*Flint*.

This word comes from the "'possum's" instinctive habit of feigning death to avoid being killed by his enemies. But with great deference to what naturalists say, and notwithstanding all the popular stories to the contrary, I am convinced that it is a habit practiced only against the dog.

A 'possum will fight a cat even unto death. I have seen it tried several times, by putting both in a large gum where they could not escape. At first the cat will have the best of it, but the 'possum will fight on without wincing till his head is a gore of blood, and at length gets his enemy by the throat or breast and holds on like a bull-dog, then nothing but timely interference will save the cat's life.

I have clubbed them, stoned them, whipped them with withes, kicked and stamped them, and even killed them in this way, just for the experiment, without any 'possuming whatever; while, sometimes, if a dog comes up and simply smells of them, and always after a snap or two, they will keel over and feign death. But it is a poor deception after all, and would not mislead anything but a dog, for instead of the stretched-out and relaxed condition of death, they are coiled up into a compact bunch. I have carried them in this condition by the tail many a time, and whenever I would gently relax my hold I would feel the prehensile action of the tail, and if I gradually let go entirely, they always took care by bending their tail around my finger not to let themselves fall. Besides, if you pull at the long hairs on the back part of their thighs, you will see them cringe at every pluck, but in other respects they will bear a great deal of punishment without flinching.

STANZA CCCCLXXV.
" Some to Galena *diggings* went."

Diggings. This word, almost always used in the plural, originally meant the place where the Indians had dug up the ground for the purpose of planting their corn, tobacco, etc. It also means the lead mines, or any mine opened by digging, and is sometimes used to designate a particular section of the country, as, "about these *diggings*," meaning about this neighborhood or about this part of the country. It is purely an Americanism.

STANZA CCCCLXXXI.
" With *wamus* well begirt."

Wamus. This word is generally written *warmus*, of which it is undoubtedly a contraction, but it is almost universally pronounced *wamus*, and so I have ventured to write it. The *wamus* resembles the well-known hunting-shirt, but differs from it in having no fringe and being worn without buttons or belt. It was girt round the waist by tying the lower corners of the skirt in front.

STANZAS CCCCLXXXIV, CCCCLXXXV.
" A friend or stranger found a home."

David Meeker came to my father's house at first to make up our shoes. After this was done he remained awhile, and made shoes for several of the neighbors and a few pairs of fine boots (he was an excellent workman) for more fashionable young men. But he still remained. At length my father's house became his home, yet not a word was ever said upon the subject of his remaining, to my knowledge. He lived with us as a member of the family for about eight years; indeed, until my father died and the family became scattered. He worked with us whenever he chose to, which was nearly always when we were at work, but never was required to do so, and we shared everything with him as if he were a brother. He was a true friend and a most amiable man.

STANZA CCCCXCII.
" Were treated as *bagasse*."

Bagasse is a French word, meaning *baggage*, as applicable to a low, worthless woman. In Louisiana it is applied to the refuse sugar-cane after it has been pressed. Its nearest synonym in English would probably be *trash*.

Whatever groveling, treacherous, or brutal traits of character there may be in the negro, I do not think that malignant hatred of other races is among them. This disposition is to be found in a higher and more ambitious people. What other race on earth than the blacks during the late war, with such an opportunity of revenging centuries of wrong, would have been so patient and forbearing?

STANZA CCCCXCIII.
Bones, banjo, quarters.

Two pieces of *bones* in each hand were used as castanets. The *banjo* is too well known to require a description. It is a rude combination of the guitar and tambourine. The name is probably a corruption of *pandero*, the Spanish word for timbrel. An instrument resembling the banjo was used by the Moors in Spain before the fifteenth century.

The huts of the slaves on the larger plantations, or any place where a considerable number of negroes lived, were called *quarters*, or *negro quarters*.

STANZA DVI.

Sharp-shin. After the war of 1812 money became very scarce, especially coin. There were but few small American coins at the time, and consequently change could hardly be had. To alleviate this inconvenience silver coins were cut into pieces, generally into an even number of equal parts. These were called *sharp-shins*, probably from the sharp point opposite the segment, and were current from necessity. The practice did not work well, however: it afforded too many facilities for *clipping* the coin.

Shin-plasters were tickets issued, generally by corporations, sometimes by individuals, to pass as money in the way of change. The *shin-plaster* proper is for some fractional part of a dollar, but the word is also sometimes applied to irredeemable or fraudulent bank-paper.

STANZA DVIII.
" Our court-house with its cupola
Was once the old ox-mill. '

This is simply the record of a fact.

STANZA DXV.

"And when we to the city went."

Every country boy will vividly remember his confusion on entering a great city for the first time, and nothing will strike his mind more forcibly than the contrast between the general splendor and gayety which prevails, and the squalor, degradation, and abject poverty seen in certain places; neither of which, in such extremes, is found in the country. And the pursuits of chimney-sweeping, street-cleaning, and rag-picking, so strange to him, leave a deep impression on his memory. He feels as if he was walled in and wanted breath, and soon sighs for the free action and fresh air of his country home.

STANZA DXXXVI.

It is said that Washington, in his youth, wrote his name higher on the rock of the Natural Bridge in Virginia than any other person, and the story is told that afterwards an ambitious youth, in attempting to place his name above Washington's, fell dead at the foot of the precipice.

STANZA DXLIX.

"The *sycamore* that braves the storm,
Wailing like troubled ghost."

The middle-sized sycamore-tree, say three feet in diameter, during the prevalence of winds, gives out a peculiar, mournful, wailing sound. It may be owing to the wind-shaken condition of its trunk, but I have never heard the same sound from any other kind of a tree.

"The *buckeye*,—though so vile and mean,—
The harbinger of spring."

The *buckeye* (*Pavia lutea*) is the first to show its green leaves in the spring along the rich bottoms. It is generally described by writers on the subject as a small tree. In this I think they are mistaken. The Ohio *buckeye* (*Pavia Ohioensis*) grows very large, especially along the Scioto River. They are found quite frequently three feet in diameter, and eighty or ninety feet in height. In the year 1836, I think it was, General Tom Worthington took to Cincinnati the section of a *buckeye*-tree, measuring six feet in diameter, upon which he stood and delivered a public address.

STANZA DLVI.

"And fight their battles o'er the clouds."

The battle of Lookout Mountain was fought above the clouds, in open sunlight.

www.ingramcontent.com/pod-product-compliance
Lightning Source LLC
Chambersburg PA
CBHW021839230426
43669CB00008B/1019